THE PASSOVER HAGGADAH OF QUESTIONS & ANSWERS

BY ALAN LANDAU

The Passover Haggadah of Questions & Answers

Published and distributed by:
Ktav Publishers and Distributers Inc.
527 Empire Boulevard
Brooklyn, NY 11225
USA
www.ktav.com
orders@ktav.com

The Hebrew text of the Haggadah is used by permission of HaOtiyot HaKetanot.
www.haotiyot.com
Typeset by Chaykee Mor.
Cover design and artwork by Chaykee Mor.

ISBN: 978-1-60280-534-7

Printed in the United States.

And it will come to pass if your children say to you,	וְהָיָה כִּי־יֹאמְרוּ אֲלֵיכֶם בְּנֵיכֶם,
What is this service to you?	מָה הָעֲבֹדָה הַזֹּאת לָכֶם?
And you shall say,	וַאֲמַרְתֶּם:
“It is a Passover sacrifice to the Lord,	זֶבַח־פֶּסַח הוּא לַיהֹוָה,
for He passed over the houses of the children of Israel	אֲשֶׁר פָּסַח עַל־בָּתֵּי בְנֵי־יִשְׂרָאֵל
in Egypt when He smote the Egyptians,	בְּמִצְרַיִם בְּנָגְפּוֹ אֶת־מִצְרַיִם,
and He saved our houses.”	וְאֶת־בָּתֵּינוּ הִצִּיל.
Exodus 12:26-27	שמות יב כו-כז

TABLE OF CONTENTS

TABLE OF CONTENTS

Dedicated with love to my children,
Lev Aryeh, Aliyah Chava and May Eden.
May you continue to learn,
so that you too may teach your children.

lively conversation, but to inspire you religiously and satisfy you intellectually. Although answers are offered, participants are encouraged to think up their own answers. This Haggadah aims to create a dialogue, rather than merely to "tell" the story.

How is this Haggadah laid out differently from other Haggadot?

I have made the decision to place the Questions & Answers directly in the body of the Haggadah text itself, breaking up the flow of the Haggadah. A strict adherence to convention would have placed the Q&A at the bottom of pages as footnotes. However, placing them there might have caused the reader to no more than glance at them or ignore them altogether. By including the Q&A directly within the body of the Haggadah text, I call on the reader to engage with them. On the night of the seder, questions should not be avoided, but highlighted.

While this Haggadah is formatted in the style of a Hebrew language book, with the spine on the right-hand side, the Q&A is laid out in the style of an English language book. This means that when the book is open, the Q&A proceeds from the left-hand page to the right-hand page. Given that this book opens like a Hebrew language book, where you might expect the Q&A to proceed from the right-hand page to the left-hand page, this may take a bit of time to get used to. Nevertheless, once it is open, I believe that this layout choice will feel more natural to readers whose first language is English.

I have chosen to lay out the English translation of the Haggadah text on the right-hand page, and the Hebrew text on left-hand page, with each line of Hebrew text matching to the corresponding English translation on the same line. Hebrew-only readers and English-only readers should not find their enjoyment impaired. I hope that English readers who understand Hebrew at any level will find their enjoyment improved, as they can quickly and easily see the translations of the Hebrew, which are often shorter and punchier, juxtaposed against what are often more verbose English translations.

To set off and highlight Shabbat-related text from the regular Haggadah text, I have chosen to use a gray-tone font. Where the Shabbat-related text amounts to an entire sentence or whole paragraph, the text is preceded by an instruction note. As with all instruction notes in this Haggadah, Shabbat-related instruction notes are visibly set out in a smaller, italicized font. However, in cases where only a few Shabbat-related words are required to be added to the Haggadah text, in order not to disrupt the flow, the Shabbat-related text is simply in a gray-tone font surrounded by parentheses, and not preceded by any instruction note.

In general, I have used a more literal translation of the Hebrew, avoiding more ornate English. In many cases, this has required inserting additional words or phrases in brackets. When used in the Haggadah text, these bracketed words and phrases are meant to clarify the text. Parentheticals in the Haggadah text are used only for the insertion of additional words required by the liturgy, for example, if a minyan is present when saying Grace after the Meal or where the text in the parenthetical is used only on Shabbat.

***

I owe a debt of gratitude to the many people who took the time to review drafts of this Haggadah over the years. I especially wish to thank my wife, Karen Orah, who graciously tolerated the many hours I devoted to this project, which took on a life of its own far beyond what I, or she, initially expected.

And thank you to the reader for using this Haggadah. I hope that you will come away not only with new knowledge, but with a renewed interest to learn more about this most important of holidays.

Alan Landau
Hong Kong 2024 (5785)

INTRODUCTION

How is this Haggadah different from other Haggadot?

The modern Jewish world is one in which non-observance, secularism, and assimilation are all too prevalent. Many Jews attend synagogue infrequently, or not at all. Yet, participation in a seder is almost universal. It is the most observed Jewish ritual. The seder brings together young and old, men and women, religious and secular, family and friends.

While there are several "musts" in a seder, including telling the story of the Exodus, singing Dayeinu, eating matzah, and searching for the Afikoman, no part is more associated with the seder than the Mah Nishtanah, the Four Questions. Almost every Jew has childhood memories of standing on a chair singing the Four Questions solo, or of singing them along with young siblings and cousins, or with a tableful of relatives of all ages – sometimes in perfect harmony, but often in a joyous, off-key cacophony! For parents and grandparents, hearing children and grandchildren sing the Mah Nishtanah marks a highlight of the evening, one that is a source of emotional poignancy and satisfaction.

If the seder is the most central religious ritual in modern Jewish life, then the Four Questions are the most central part of this most central ritual. Much of the Haggadah is essentially a response, providing answers, albeit obtusely, to them. Yet, for too many Jews, the Haggadah is almost as impenetrable as a tractate of the Mishnah, that cryptic compendium of Jewish oral law. As much as memories of seders past may be filled with recollections of singing the Four Questions, for too many Jews, memories of boredom and genuine confusion are even more vivid.

Modern Haggadot have attempted different ways to make the seder more engaging. Some change the wording to be more inclusive and egalitarian, while others add additional texts, or even cut out whole swaths of the traditional text altogether. Other Haggadot provide games and distractions. Among those Haggadot that adhere to the traditional text, another common approach is to include stories and explanations of a historic, religious, or moral nature. What all these Haggadot tend to have in common is a passive approach to telling the story of the Exodus.

It is true that we are commanded to "tell" [וְהִגַּדְתָּ] our children about the Exodus from Egypt. Yet, it is not enough simply to tell our children the story, let alone just to read about it from the Haggadah. Rather, whether there are children at the table who know nothing about Passover, or the whole table is full of Torah scholars well versed in all the ritual, legal and historical matters related to Passover, we are meant to ask questions and discuss.

What makes this Haggadah different from other Haggadot is that it focuses on clarifying the purpose, meaning and historical context of many aspects of the seder, the Exodus, and the Haggadah itself, by offering questions to stimulate thinking and participation. Questions are offered ranging from simple ones, to which most children will be able to offer a response, to more esoteric questions, which will be a challenge for even the most knowledgeable to answer, and everything in between. Uniquely, this Haggadah does not shy away from controversial questions, including the historicity of the Exodus itself and the origins of many of the customs that are a part of the seder.

With more than 170 questions, there are more than can be covered in several seders, much less one. It is my hope that you will continue to return to this Haggadah again and again, not only to stimulate

What does "*Haggadah*" mean?

The word "*Haggadah*" means "telling", but also can be translated as "relating", "recounting", "declaring" or "proclaiming". We read from a *Haggadah* because of the commandment in the Book of Exodus stating "You shall tell [וְהִגַּדְתָּ] your child that day" about going out from Egypt. Following the Exodus, the Jewish people were commanded to tell the story of the Exodus to their children. Over many generations, the *Haggadah* was assembled as a guidebook for how to fulfill this commandment.

Why is this holiday called Passover?

After more than 200 years of slavery, God heard the suffering of the Israelites, and remembered His promise to Abraham, Isaac and Jacob to give their descendants the land of Canaan. Pharaoh would not willingly let the Israelites go free, so God brought a series of plagues down on Egypt, the last of which was the killing of the firstborn. To spare the firstborn of the Israelites, God commanded that they paint their doorposts with the blood of a sacrificial lamb, which would act as a sign to the Angel of Death to "pass over" the homes of the Israelites.

What are other names for the Passover holiday? And why go by these names?

Passover is called *Chag HaMatzot*, Festival of *Matzot*, because we are forbidden to eat *chametz* during Passover. During the seven days of Passover (or eight days outside the Land of Israel), we may only eat *matzah* in place of leavened products. There is also a deeper meaning in the idea of the word '*matzah*'. Whereas *chametz* is leavened, *matzah* is flat. *Chametz* is therefore associated with arrogance, while *matzah* is associated with humbleness. There is a further association with humbleness and Passover, because the Torah calls Moses an "exceedingly humble" man.

Passover is called *Chag HaAviv*, Festival of Spring, because the Torah directly associates Passover with spring. Spring is associated with rebirth and renewal. Just as spring redeems the world from the symbolic death of winter, the Exodus redeemed the Jewish people from the symbolic death of slavery.

Passover is called *Chag HaPesach*, Festival of the Passover Offering, because God commanded the children of Israel to make a Passover offering of a lamb, the blood of which was placed on the doorposts of their homes to avert the killing of the firstborn. However, the blood was more than just a sign of protection from the tenth and final plague; it contained a deeper meaning. The lamb was associated with the Egyptian god, Khnemu, a god of fertility. Therefore, the sacrifice of the lamb as the Passover offering was a visible symbol of the Israelites' faith in God, and His triumph over the Egyptians' gods.

Passover is called *Zman Cheruteinu*, Season of Our Freedom, because it was at this holiday that the Jewish people were redeemed from slavery in Egypt and became a free people under the kingship of God. The story of the Exodus is not only a central aspect of the *seder*, but it is also a cornerstone of Judaism. We are commanded in the Torah to remember the Exodus and to teach it to our children, and we continually remind ourselves of it during our daily prayers. One of Judaism's great innovations as a religion was the belief that God is a God of History. Whereas ancient gods personified natural forces that were capricious and arbitrary, Judaism teaches that God cares about the Jewish people. He heard our suffering in Egypt and He fulfilled a personal promise. At Passover we recognize that it was at this time that God brought our ancestors out of Egypt, from slavery to freedom, and in so doing He redeemed every one of us.

What is the message of Passover?

Passover is more than just a ritual. It is an act of remembering – not just of the Exodus itself, but of the lived historical experience that flowed throughout the generations following that event. It is through this act of remembering that we join together, not only with those around the *seder* table, but with all

Q&A

How do we know the Exodus happened?

The Exodus is more than a just a story. It is the central narrative that explains who the Jewish people are, our place in the world, and our relationship with God. Yet for many Biblical scholars it is nothing more than a post hoc etiological myth written as part of Jewish history building. Such scholars note that there is no direct evidence of hundreds of thousands, much less millions of Israelites escaping Egyptian slavery. They argue that because neither hieroglyphics or other contemporary corroborative testimony describing an enslavement or escape, nor any remains of any encampments or signs of a mass scale movement of peoples in the Sinai desert have been found, the Exodus must not have occurred. Absence of evidence, they argue, is evidence of absence.

The traditional Rabbinic response to this question has focused on the simple faith that the Torah was handed from God to Moses, and from Moses on along an unbroken line across generations without any alteration. According to this line of thinking, since the Torah is true and has been passed through this chain unaltered, then the story of the Exodus contained therein must also be true. However, most secular people doubt the premises upon which the conclusion is based. Another religious approach, focusing more on logic, is based on the nature of the Exodus and the revelation at Sinai. Unlike other religions, which were founded by a single man and his singular experience, the founding of Judaism through the Exodus and at Sinai was a collective experience. It may be possible to fool one man, and for one man to fool another, but 603,550 adult men could not all be fooled!

Yet neither faith nor logic need be relied upon. Both secular and religious scholars are increasingly recognizing hints inside the Torah, and from the archeological record, that attest to the historicity of the Exodus. Professor Joshua Berman notes that the Torah describes God saving the Israelites "with a strong hand and outstretched arm", a phrase which outside the Book of Exodus is used only by Egyptian texts in describing the might of Pharaoh. Professor Berman also notes other examples where the Torah appropriates from Egypt, including the layout of the *Mishkan* (the portable sanctuary used in the desert), which mirrors Pharaoh Ramses II's war tent. Even the Hebrews' complaints in the desert when they longingly remembered the "onions and garlic" they ate "free of charge" demonstrates specific knowledge of Egyptian slave life. Professors Edwin Yamauchi and Marvin Wilson have demonstrated that onions and garlic were popular vegetables in ancient Egypt and were part of the wages that workers on the Great Pyramid of Giza received. All these examples suggest an intimate familiarity with Egyptian culture that makes little sense if the Jewish people had never been in Egypt.

Further, while Professor James Kugel and Professor Richard Elliott Friedman both cast doubt on the scale of the Exodus, each offers abundant evidence that shows that the Jewish people were in Egypt. Among the evidence they offer: many of the names of the Israelites mentioned in the Exodus story are of Egyptian origin (including Moses, Phineas, Miriam and others); the repetitive focus (52 times) on the treatment of the "stranger"; the commandment to circumcise (which was a common Egyptian ritual not practiced in Canaan); and detailed knowledge of Egyptian fortifications and sites that would have been unknown if the story had been written many years after the events described.

Language provides another example attesting to a Jewish presence in Egypt that goes beyond simple, secondhand knowledge. Dr. Benjamin J. Noonan notes that the *Tanach* contains more than 70 loan words from Egyptian. Yet these loan words occur 12 times as often in the Exodus and wilderness narratives than they occur in all the rest of the *Tanach* combined.

Ultimately, the centrality of the Exodus to the Jewish tradition makes answering the question of its historicity an important one. Whether based upon faith, logic, or empirical evidence, a Jew of any level of religious observance can confidently state that the Exodus happened.

ruling in our own land, and speaking the very same language. This was only possible because God cared about the Israelite slaves, what He called the "smallest" people. That is a powerful message of hope for the world, and should be a wakeup call for those people who would abuse their wealth and power.

Why does the word "freedom" not appear in the story of the Exodus?

The Haggadah speaks of "freedom", but the narrative of the Exodus in the Torah never uses the word. While the Israelites were redeemed from slavery, they were not redeemed to freedom. Rather they were redeemed to the service of God. As if to make this point clear, the Torah frames the ultimate redemptive act, the killing of the firstborn, which causes Pharaoh to free the Israelites from bondage, with the giving of laws. First, immediately before the tenth plague, the law of the new month (which is necessary for calculating the calendar and the observance of festivals) and the law of the Passover offering (which commemorates the deliverance from slavery) are given. Immediately following the tenth plague and the Exodus, the laws regarding redemption of the firstborn, remembering the Exodus, and *tefillin* are given. Getting the Israelites out of Egypt – the redemption from slavery – was only one step in the journey. Getting the Egypt out of the Israelites – and us – is the ultimate goal. By providing the former slaves and their descendants a set of laws, God is telling us that the Jewish people were not redeemed to be free. Rather, they – and we – were redeemed to become a holy people, a people acting righteously to others and obediently to God. This requires rules, statutes and laws. True freedom is living an ordered life by serving a higher purpose.

Jews, throughout all time, and connect with our past. In fact, the word *Haggadah* is also related to the Hebrew word "gid" [גיד], meaning "tendon", the sinew that binds and connects bones to muscle. Thus, the Haggadah can be seen as binding and connecting us through the seder's rituals to all those Jews who came before us, back to the Exodus itself. No matter where you come from, what country you live in, what language you speak, or your background, the Passover story is for all of us.

However, Passover is more than simply remembering and connecting with the past. This is clear from the *Haggadah*'s clarion call: "Now we are slaves, next year we shall be free". If it was only about the past, we might say, "We were slaves, but now we are free". Moving from slavery to freedom did not just happen at a static moment in time, but is rather a continuing process, which we too are part of. We are called upon to act to build our future. It is within our capacity to move from slavery to freedom, both literal and metaphoric. And this message is not only for the Jewish people. It is universally applicable to all Mankind. There are still people who are not free, and those of us who are, cannot truly be while others are enslaved.

Another important message is that it is not wealth or power that matter most, but what we do with the wealth and power that we have. Egypt was surely the wealthiest and most powerful nation at the time of the Exodus. If anyone at that time considered who would be around in 3000 years – the Egyptians and their gods, culture and language, or the Hebrew slaves and their God, culture, and language – the answer would have been obvious: surely the mighty Egyptians would endure and the lowly Hebrew slaves would disappear. Yet, it is we, the Jewish people, who are still here, worshiping the same God,

PESACH PREPARATIONS

The Search For Chametz

After nightfall on the 14th of Nissan (the night before the first night of Passover), as soon as possible following evening prayers, begin the search for chametz. If the 14th of Nissan falls on erev Shabbat, conduct the search for chametz after nightfall on the 13th of Nissan. Place ten small, wrapped pieces of chametz (no more than a k'zayit each) around the home where they can be easily found. Traditionally, the search is conducted by the light of a beeswax candle, using a wooden spoon and feather to collect the chametz into a paper bag.

Before beginning the search, recite the following blessing.

Blessed are You, Lord, our God, King of the universe,
who has sanctified us with His commandments
and commanded us concerning the disposal chametz.

After the search is completed, place the chametz (as well as the spoon, feather, candle and paper bag, if used, together with the chametz) in a safe place until the following morning.

Recite the following in Aramaic, only if understood, if not, recite in English:

All leaven and leavened products that are in my possession,
which I did not observe, did not dispose of, or do not know about,
are hereby nullified and ownerless, like the dust of the earth.

The Burning of the Chametz

On the following morning, generally no later than 10 am, burn the chametz (including the paper bag, feather, and spoon, if used), as well as any other chametz in your possession.

After placing the chametz in fire, recite the following in Aramaic, only if understood, if not, recite in English:

All leaven and leavened products that are in my possession,
which I did or did not see, which I did or did not observe,
which I did or did not dispose of,
are hereby nullified and ownerless, like the dust of the earth.

Why do we conduct the search by the light of a candle?

The Talmud teaches that conducting the search by candle is preferable to using a torch, which, prior to electricity, were the only available light sources. A torch was considered impractical given that one cannot easily hold it close enough to one's face to carefully conduct the search. A somewhat indirect scriptural support for using a candle is found in the book of Proverbs, which states "I will search Jerusalem with candles." This suggested to the sages that a candle is the appropriate tool to use to find something. However, some rabbis hold that any light is acceptable to conduct the search by, including flashlights and other electronic light sources.

הכנה לפסח

בדיקת חמץ

After nightfall on the 14th of ניסן (the night before the first night of פסח), as soon as possible following evening prayers, begin the search for חמץ. If the 14th of ניסן falls on ערב שבת, conduct the search for חמץ after nightfall on the 13th of ניסן. Place ten small, wrapped pieces of חמץ (no more than a כזית each) around the home where they can be easily found. Traditionally, the search is conducted by the light of a beeswax candle, using a wooden spoon and feather to collect the חמץ into a paper bag.

Before beginning the search, recite the following ברכה.

בָּרוּךְ אַתָּה יְהֹוָה אֱלֹהֵינוּ מֶלֶךְ הָעוֹלָם,
אֲשֶׁר קִדְּשָׁנוּ בְּמִצְוֹתָיו
וְצִוָּנוּ עַל בִּעוּר חָמֵץ.

After the search is completed, place the חמץ (as well as the spoon, feather, candle and paper bag, if used, together with the חמץ) in a safe place until the following morning.

Recite the following in Aramaic, only if understood, if not, recite in English:

כָּל חֲמִירָא וַחֲמִיעָא דְּאִכָּא בִרְשׁוּתִי,
דְּלָא חֲזִתֵּיהּ וּדְלָא בִעַרְתֵּיהּ וּדְלָא יְדַעְנָא לֵיהּ,
לִבָּטֵל וְלֶהֱוֵי הֶפְקֵר כְּעַפְרָא דְאַרְעָא.

ביעור חמץ

On the following morning, generally no later than 10 am, burn the חמץ (including the paper bag, feather, and spoon, if used), as well as any other חמץ in your possession.

After placing the חמץ in fire, recite the following in Aramaic, only if understood, if not, recite in English:

כָּל חֲמִירָא וַחֲמִיעָא דְּאִכָּא בִרְשׁוּתִי,
דַּחֲזִתֵּהּ וּדְלָא חֲזִתֵּהּ דַּחֲמִתֵּהּ וּדְלָא חֲמִתֵּהּ,
דְּבִעַרְתֵּהּ וּדְלָא בִעַרְתֵּהּ,
לִבָּטֵל וְלֶהֱוֵי הֶפְקֵר כְּעַפְרָא דְאַרְעָא.

Q&A

Why do we search for *chametz*?

The prohibition regarding *chametz* is different from any other food-related law. So absolute is the prohibition that the Torah states in respect of anyone who eats *chametz* during Passover, "that soul will be cut off from the community of Israel." To avoid transgressing, the Torah therefore prohibits even owning *chametz*. Consequently, we are scrupulous in cleaning our home in the days and weeks before the holiday to ensure that it is totally free of any *chametz*. To be absolutely certain that our home contains no *chametz*, the night before Passover begins, we conduct a final search to find any that may have been missed while cleaning the home.

Why do we conduct the search using a wooden spoon and feather?

The feather is used as a broom to sweep the *chametz* onto the spoon, which acts as the receptacle. Because these items have come in contact with *chametz*, they too must be burned the following morning. A wooden spoon and feather are easily burned, and have therefore been the traditional implements with which to conduct the search.

Eruv Tavshilin

When the second day of Passover falls on Shabbat or if Shabbat begins immediately after Passover, prepare two types of food, one cooked (no smaller than a large olive) and one baked (about the size of a chicken egg) and set them aside.

Before the start of Passover, hold them aloft and say the following blessing and text in Aramaic. If you do not understand Aramaic, recite it in English.

Blessed are You, Lord, our God, King of the universe,
who has sanctified us with His commandments
and commanded us concerning the mitzvah of eruv.

By means of this eruv it will be permissible
to bake, cook, keep dishes warm, to kindle a light [from an existing flame],
and to prepare and do all our necessities
on the festival for the needs of Shabbat,
for us and all Jews who live in this city.

The two food items must remain intact throughout the time preparations are made for Shabbat. Eat them on Shabbat.

---

holiday preparations. A second reason is that the ritual acts as a formal reminder that although preparing food for Shabbat is permitted on the holiday, preparing food on the holiday for the regular week is strictly prohibited.

What if the *eruv tavshilin* is not done?

So long as the *eruv tavshilin* was not forgotten due to negligence, one may rely upon the *eruv tavshilin* performed by a rabbi in the community, as it is incumbent upon him to have his community in mind when performing the ritual.

Why do we place *chametz* around the home in preparation for the search?

Ideally, because of the careful cleaning of the home prior to the start of the holiday, there should be no *chametz*. Therefore, we place *chametz* around the home so the search will not be done in vain.

עירוב תבשילין

When the second day of פסח falls on שבת or if שבת begins immediately after פסח, prepare two types of food, one cooked (no smaller than a large olive) and one baked (about the size of a chicken egg) and set them aside.

Before the start of פסח, hold them aloft and say the following ברכה and text in Aramaic. If you do not understand Aramaic, recite it in English.

בָּרוּךְ אַתָּה יְהֹוָה אֱלֹהֵינוּ מֶלֶךְ הָעוֹלָם,
אֲשֶׁר קִדְּשָׁנוּ בְּמִצְוֹתָיו
וְצִוָּנוּ עַל מִצְוַת עֵירוּב.

בַּהֲדֵין עֵרוּבָא יְהֵא שָׁרָא לָנָא
לַאֲפוּיֵי וּלְבַשּׁוּלֵי וּלְאַטְמוּנֵי וּלְאַדְלוּקֵי שְׁרָגָא,
וּלְתַּ וּלְתַקָּנָא וּלְמֶעְבַּד כָּל צָרְכָנָא
מִיּוֹמָא טָבָא לְשַׁבַּתָּא,
לָנָא וּלְכָל יִשְׂרָאֵל הַדָּרִים בָּעִיר הַזֹּאת.

The two food items must remain intact throughout the time preparations are made for שבת. Eat them on שבת.

What is an *eruv tavshilin*?

When the second day of a holiday falls on Shabbat or if Shabbat begins immediately after a holiday, it is rabbinically forbidden to prepare food for Shabbat on the holiday. An *eruv tavshilin* is a ritual that renders this prohibition void, thereby permitting the preparation of Shabbat food on the holiday.

Why is an *eruv tavshilin* needed?

Although there is no prohibition in the Torah against preparing Shabbat food on a holiday, two reasons are offered by the sages in the Talmud. The first reason is to provide a tangible reminder that preparations for Shabbat must be done before the start of the holiday, lest the Shabbat be overlooked due to the

CANDLE LIGHTING

For the first (and seventh) night, while candle lighting should be done 18 minutes before sunset, it may be delayed. However, if candle lighting is delayed past sunset, the candles must be lit from a pre-existing flame.
In addition, on the second (and eighth) day of the festival, or if the festival begins immediately after Shabbat, candle lighting must be done after the appearance of three stars, and the candles must be lit from a pre-existing flame.

Recite the following blessing:

Blessed are You, Lord, our God, King of the universe,
who has sanctified us with His commandments
and commanded us to kindle the (Shabbat and) festival lights.

For the first (and second) night, say the following blessing:

Blessed are You, Lord, our God, King of the universe,
who has granted us life, sustained us, and enabled us to reach this [special] time.

Following the lighting of the candles, women traditionally offer the following blessing.

הדלקת נרות

For the first (and seventh) night, while candle lighting should be done 18 minutes before sunset, it may be delayed. However, if candle lighting is delayed past sunset, the candles must be lit from a pre-existing flame. In addition, on the second (and eighth) day of the festival, or if the festival begins immediately after שבת*, candle lighting must be done after the appearance of three stars, and the candles must be lit from a pre-existing flame.*

Recite the following ברכה*:*

בָּרוּךְ אַתָּה יְהֹוָה אֱלֹהֵינוּ מֶלֶךְ הָעוֹלָם,
אֲשֶׁר קִדְּשָׁנוּ בְּמִצְוֹתָיו
וְצִוָּנוּ לְהַדְלִיק נֵר שֶׁל (שַׁבָּת וְשֶׁל) יוֹם טוֹב.

For the first (and second) night, say the following ברכה*:*

בָּרוּךְ אַתָּה יְהֹוָה אֱלֹהֵינוּ מֶלֶךְ הָעוֹלָם,
שֶׁהֶחֱיָנוּ וְקִיְּמָנוּ וְהִגִּיעָנוּ לַזְּמַן הַזֶּה.

Following the lighting of the candles, women traditionally offer the following ברכה*.*

It is the custom of some to offer other, personal prayers.

May it be your will before You,
Lord, my God, God of Israel,
to be gracious to me and to my husband,
and to my sons and to my daughters, and to all who are close to me.
And grant us and all Israel a good and long life,
and remember us for good and blessing
and consider us for salvation and mercy,
and may Your presence dwell among us.
And may we be privileged to raise wise and understanding children and grandchildren,
who love the Lord and fear God,
truthful people, holy offspring, attached to the Lord,
and who enlighten the world with Torah and good deeds,
and in service to the Creator.
Please hear my prayers,
in the merit of Sarah, Rebecca, Rachel and Leah, our matriarchs,
and ensure the light of their lives will never be dimmed,
and show us Your face so that we may be saved. Amen.

Why do we wave our hands and cover our eyes before lighting the candles?

Blessings must be made before a benefit has been received. For example, we bless our food before eating it. Therefore, we cover our eyes immediately after lighting the candles to avoid deriving benefit from them. Once the blessing is complete, we uncover our eyes, and then enjoy their light. Waving our hands over the candles three times can be seen as symbolizing preparation for deriving benefit from the candles, as well as a motion representing the welcoming of the Shabbat queen.

Why do women, rather than men, traditionally light the candles?

The traditional reason for women lighting the candles, related by Rabbi Yehoshua in the *midrash*, is as a correction for Eve's sin of causing Adam to eat from the tree of good and evil. The penalty for this sin was Man's mortality, a symbolic extinguishing of light. By lighting the candles, women symbolically return light to the world. Maimonides in contrast taught that women light the candles because they are more observant than men, being engaged in duties of the home, of which lighting the candles is one such duty. A more egalitarian explanation, which is nevertheless consistent with Jewish tradition, is that women are likened to the Shabbat queen, bringing light and Torah into the home. Lighting the candles is therefore symbolic of this role.

It is the custom of some to offer other, personal prayers.

יְהִי רָצוֹן מִלְּפָנֶיךָ,
יְהוָה אֱלֹהַי וֵאלֹהֵי יִשְׂרָאֵל,
שֶׁתְּחוֹנֵן אוֹתִי וְאֶת אִישִׁי,
וְאֶת בָּנַי וּבְנוֹתַי וְאֶת כָּל קְרוֹבַי.
וְתִתֵּן לָנוּ וּלְכָל יִשְׂרָאֵל חַיִּים טוֹבִים וַאֲרוּכִים,
וְתִזְכְּרֵנוּ בְּזִכְרוֹן טוֹבָה וּבְרָכָה
וְתִפְקְדֵנוּ בִּפְקֻדַּת יְשׁוּעָה וְרַחֲמִים,
וְתַשְׁכֵּן שְׁכִינָתְךָ בֵּינֵינוּ.
וְזַכֵּנוּ לְגַדֵּל בָּנִים וּבְנֵי בָנִים חֲכָמִים וּנְבוֹנִים,
אוֹהֲבֵי יְהוָה, יִרְאֵי אֱלֹהִים,
אַנְשֵׁי אֱמֶת, זֶרַע קֹדֶשׁ, בַּיהוָה דְּבֵקִים,
וּמְאִירִים אֶת הָעוֹלָם בַּתּוֹרָה וּבְמַעֲשִׂים טוֹבִים,
וּבְכָל מְלֶאכֶת עֲבוֹדַת הַבּוֹרֵא.
אָנָּא שְׁמַע אֶת תְּחִנָּתִי,
בִּזְכוּת שָׂרָה וְרִבְקָה, רָחֵל וְלֵאָה אִמּוֹתֵינוּ,
וְהָאֵר נֵרֵנוּ שֶׁלֹּא יִכְבֶּה לְעוֹלָם וָעֶד,
וְהָאֵר פָּנֶיךָ וְנִוָּשֵׁעָה. אָמֵן.

Q&A

Why do we light candles for Shabbat and the holidays?

The Torah expressly forbids kindling a fire on Shabbat, and this prohibition was extended by the Oral Law to the holidays. The Karaites, a Jewish sect that rejected the Oral Law, believed it was equally impermissible to have a fire burning on Shabbat, even if kindled prior to its start. Pejoratively, the Karaites are thought to sit in the dark and eat cold food on Shabbat. Our sages, perhaps in response, ruled that it was not only permissible to benefit from the light of a fire kindled before Shabbat, but in fact a positive commandment to do so. This commandment allows for the fulfillment of a verse in Isaiah that we "call Shabbat a delight". Indeed, how could anyone find delight in Shabbat ("*oneg Shabbat*") sitting in darkness and eating cold food, as the Karaites? The practice of lighting candles was a later rabbinic extension of the commandment to kindle a flame before Shabbat. Unlike that flame, however, it was forbidden to use the candlelight for practical purposes, such as for reading. Rather than being used on Shabbat for warmth and light, the candles symbolize the warmth and light of Shabbat itself.

THE SEDER PLATE

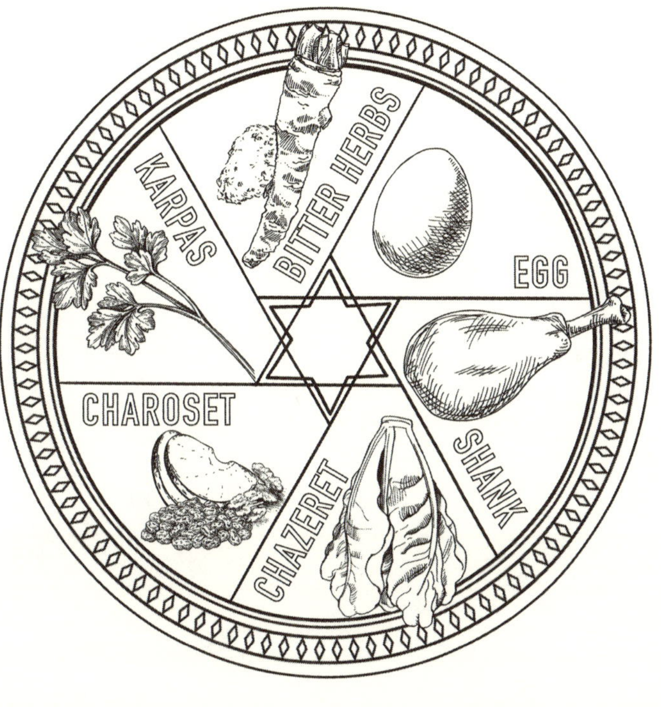

to a Midrash, when Pharoah condemned the Israelite boys to death, the Israelite men despaired having any more children, and so the women seduced them, later giving birth in the fields under apple trees. This interpretation accords with the sweetness of *charoset*, into which the bitter herbs are dipped, thus providing another example of the dualities of which the seder is replete: bitterness and sweetness, slavery and freedom, suffering and redemption, questions and answers, and past and present.

Why are there two bitter herbs?

The Torah commands that the Passover offering be eaten with "bitter herbs". The Mishnah lists five different vegetables, including *chazeret*, which qualify as a bitter herb. Only the meaning of *chazeret* is reasonably clear. The Sages understood *chazeret* to mean lettuce, and romaine lettuce came to be the commonly accepted choice. However, romaine lettuce was not easy to obtain in many parts of the world at the time of Passover, and so any bitter herb became acceptable. Horseradish, a commonly available root vegetable in Europe, is the most widely used substitute for *maror* among Ashkenazim. Although now romaine lettuce is easily obtained, the tradition of using horseradish as *maror* continues. Nevertheless, most hold that because the korech represents the commandment to eat the Passover offering with matzah and *maror*, it is best to use the *chazeret* in the Hillel sandwich.

What else is needed at the *seder* table?

Besides those items set out on the seder plate, the seder table should have three pieces of matzah, ideally shmurah matzah, covered on a plate (in addition to more matzah to be eaten by participants during the seder), as well as salt water for dipping the karpas. It has also become acceptable to have snack foods – fresh or dried fruit, candy, nuts – anything to help keep the participants from getting overly hungry and losing focus on the night's festivities.

קערת הסדר

Q&A

What does the *zeroa* represent?

Commonly a roasted chicken bone or lamb shank, *zeroa*, literally meaning "arm", symbolizes the "outstretched" arm of God, which redeemed the Jewish people from slavery. The *zeroa* is one of the two cooked dishes the sages in the Mishna mandated be presented at the seder, serving as a symbol of the Passover offering. Because it is forbidden to sacrifice outside the Temple, many have the custom not to eat the *zeroa* to avoid giving the impression of eating an actual Passover offering. Some have the custom of using a beet in place of a roasted bone, both to avoid any confusion with an actual Passover offering, as well as because the deep red color can be seen as symbolizing the sacrificial blood.

What does the egg represent?

The egg, usually roasted, is one of the two cooked dishes the sages mandated be presented at the seder, and serves as a symbol of the special *Chagigah* offering brought at the three festivals: Passover, Shavuot and Sukkot. An egg is also traditionally associated with mourning and is eaten before the start of the Tisha B'Av fast. Tisha B'Av, which commemorates the destruction of the two Temples, always falls on the same day of the week as the first day of Passover. So, the egg serves as a reminder of the destruction of the Temple and symbolizes the loss of the sacrificial offerings. Looked at more positively, an egg is a symbol of the cycle of life, and therefore connected to the idea of rebirth, a concept associated with Passover as the Festival of Spring.

What does the *charoset* represent?

Although it is not mentioned in the Torah, *charoset*, a blend of nuts, apples and wine, is mentioned in the Mishnah. According to Rabbi Yochanan, the *charoset* represents the mortar used by the Israelites in their slave labor. Yet, *charoset* is sweet, and hardly a fitting reminder for the suffering of the Israelites in slavery. In the same Mishnah, Rabbi Levi says that *charoset* represents the apple. What apple? According

ORDER OF THE SEDER

It is popular to sing the order of the seder in Hebrew, which is in the form of a poem written by a medieval French rabbi, Rabbeinu Shmuel, called "Kadesh Urchatz".

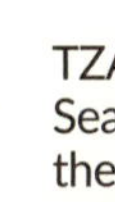

KADESH
Bless the
First Cup

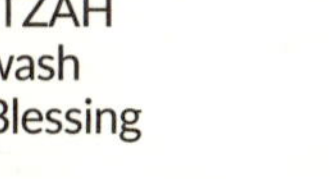

RACHTZAH
Handwash
With Blessing

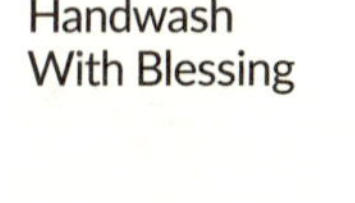

TZAFUN
Search for and Eat
the Afikoman

URCHATZ
Handwash
Without Blessing

MOTZI MATZAH
Blessings
Over Matzah

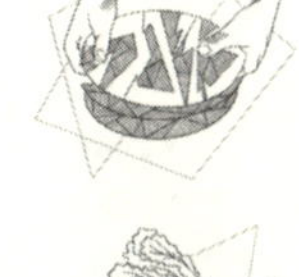

BARECH
Birkat Hamazon and
Third Cup

KARPAS
Dip the
Green Vegetable

MAROR
Dip the
Maror in Charoset

HALLEL
Psalms of Praise and
Fourth Cup

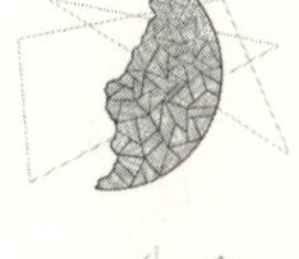

YACHATZ
Break the
Middle Matzah

KORECH
Eat the
Hillel Sandwich

NIRTZAH
Conclusion
"Next Year in Jerusalem"

MAGID
Tell the
Story of the Exodus

SHULCHAN ORECH
Eat the
Festive Meal

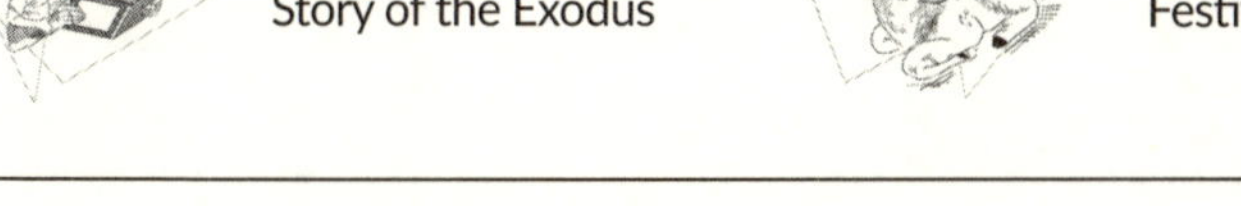

Where does the tradition of the *seder* come from?

In ancient times, the Temple in Jerusalem was the central religious site around which Jewish life revolved. The sacrificial offerings and other rituals related to the Temple followed a highly prescribed order. When the Temple stood, there were specific sacrifices which related to the Passover holiday. At that time, Passover involved the sacrifice of a lamb and the ritual eating of that lamb. However, following the destruction of the Temple, just as the synagogue and daily prayers replaced the Temple and the daily sacrificial offerings, so too the Passover *seder* came to replace the Passover sacrifices and rituals. Our *seder* only came together in the form we have today after many centuries of development by our Rabbis following the Temple's destruction.

What does "*seder*" mean? Why do we call the Passover meal and the discussions we have about Passover, a "*seder*"?

Seder literally means "order". Our Rabbis structured the *seder* evening around a set, prescribed list of things to do, just as there was a set, prescribed list of things to do in the Temple sacrifices.

סימני הסדר

It is popular to sing the order of the סדר in Hebrew, which is in the form of a poem written by a medieval French rabbi, Rabbeinu Shmuel, called "קדש ורחץ".

Q&A

What did the Rabbis who formed the modern *seder* base it upon, and how does it differ from that source?

The Rabbis of the post–Temple era modeled the Passover *seder* on the classical Greek "symposium". Symposium literally means "fellow drinker". So, it is not surprising that drinking is a central aspect of the *seder*. However, a symposium was much more than just an opportunity to get drunk. It was also a cerebral event at which philosophical topics were discussed. The discussion of the Exodus is in fact one of the main features that our Rabbis borrowed from the classical symposium, but there were many others. The Rabbis also prescribed the eating of appetizers dipped in salt water, reclining while eating, ceremonially washing the hands of others, and the *Afikoman*, all of which are features of the Greek symposium that are attested to in ancient Greek literature, including Plato's book, "Symposium". However, the *seder* is different from an ancient Greek symposium in an important way. Symposiums were hosted by aristocrats for their friends. They were just for the wealthy. Slaves were not allowed, unless they were serving the food and drinks! The Passover *seder*, in contrast, has always been for everyone, including the poor, the young, women, the uneducated, and even strangers. This is a powerful message of inclusion and teaches us that all members of the community have a place in it, and everyone can add to it.

SHABBAT EVE

Welcoming the Angels

On Shabbat, begin here.

If Shabbat falls on a seder night, sing each stanza once.
If Shabbat falls on Chol HaMoed, sing each stanza three times.

Peace be upon you ministering angels, angels of the Most High One,
messengers of the King of kings, the Holy One, blessed is He.

Come in peace you ministering angels, angels of the Most High One,
messengers of the King of kings, the Holy One, blessed is He.

Bless me in peace ministering angels, angels of the Most High One,
messengers of the King of kings, the Holy One, blessed is He.

Go in peace you ministering angels, angels of the Most High One,
messengers of the King of kings, the Holy One, blessed is He.

How and why does the Sephardic version of *Shalom Aleichem* differ from this version?

Sephardic Jews traditionally precede the last verse with:

בְּשִׁבְתְּכם לְשָׁלוֹם	May you stay in peace
מַלְאֲכֵי הַשָּׁלוֹם מַלְאֲכֵי עֶלְיוֹן	you ministering angels, angels of the Most High One,
מִמֶּלֶךְ מַלְכֵי הַמְּלָכִים הַקָּדוֹשׁ בָּרוּךְ הוּא	messengers of the King of kings, the Holy One, blessed is He.

The view held among Sephardic Jews is that the final verse, "Go in peace", seems to be encouraging the angels to leave. The inclusion of the verse, "May you stay in peace", therefore resolves this complaint.

ליל שבת

שלום עליכם

On Shabbat, begin here.

If שבת falls on a סדר night, sing each stanza once.
If שבת falls on חול המועד, sing each stanza three times.

שָׁלוֹם עֲלֵיכֶם מַלְאֲכֵי הַשָּׁרֵת מַלְאֲכֵי עֶלְיוֹן,
מִמֶּלֶךְ מַלְכֵי הַמְּלָכִים הַקָּדוֹשׁ בָּרוּךְ הוּא.

בּוֹאֲכֶם לְשָׁלוֹם מַלְאֲכֵי הַשָּׁלוֹם מַלְאֲכֵי עֶלְיוֹן,
מִמֶּלֶךְ מַלְכֵי הַמְּלָכִים הַקָּדוֹשׁ בָּרוּךְ הוּא.

בָּרְכוּנִי לְשָׁלוֹם מַלְאֲכֵי הַשָּׁלוֹם מַלְאֲכֵי עֶלְיוֹן,
מִמֶּלֶךְ מַלְכֵי הַמְּלָכִים הַקָּדוֹשׁ בָּרוּךְ הוּא.

צֵאתְכֶם לְשָׁלוֹם מַלְאֲכֵי הַשָּׁלוֹם מַלְאֲכֵי עֶלְיוֹן,
מִמֶּלֶךְ מַלְכֵי הַמְּלָכִים הַקָּדוֹשׁ בָּרוּךְ הוּא.

What is the meaning of *Shalom Aleichem*?

The phrase *"shalom aleichem"* means "peace be upon you". The Talmud relates that when a person returns home from *Kabbalat Shabbat* services Friday evening, he is accompanied by two angels, one good and one bad. If the angels arrive at a peaceful home beautifully set for Shabbat, the good angel blesses the home for it to be so again the following week, and the bad angel is forced to affirm this blessing with an "amen". This song welcomes these angels, calls upon them to bless us, and then wishes them to go in peace. Just as we greet fellow Jews with "*shalom aleichem*", the kabbalists who wrote the song metaphorically call upon us to greet the angels that accompany us at the Shabbat table.

A Woman of Valor

A Woman of Valor who can find?
Her value far exceeds pearls.
Her husband trusts her in his heart,
and he lacks no gain.
She does good by him, never evil,
all the days of her life.
She seeks wool and flax,
and sets her hand working willingly.
She is like the merchant fleet,
bringing food from afar.
She arises while it still night,
and gives food to her household, and a portion to her maids.
She sets her mind to a field and acquires it,
she plants a vineyard with the work of her hands.
She girds her loins with strength,
and makes her arms strong.
She perceives that her business thrives,
her lamp does not go out at night.
She lays her hand on the distaff,
and her hand holds the spindle.

אשת חיל

אֵשֶׁת חַיִל מִי יִמְצָא?
וְרָחֹק מִפְּנִינִים מִכְרָהּ.
בָּטַח בָּהּ לֵב בַּעְלָהּ,
וְשָׁלָל לֹא יֶחְסָר.
גְּמָלַתְהוּ טוֹב וְלֹא רָע,
כֹּל יְמֵי חַיֶּיהָ.
דָּרְשָׁה צֶמֶר וּפִשְׁתִּים,
וַתַּעַשׂ בְּחֵפֶץ כַּפֶּיהָ.
הָיְתָה כָּאֳנִיּוֹת סוֹחֵר,
מִמֶּרְחָק תָּבִיא לַחְמָהּ.
וַתָּקָם בְּעוֹד לַיְלָה,
וַתִּתֵּן טֶרֶף לְבֵיתָהּ וְחֹק לְנַעֲרֹתֶיהָ.
זָמְמָה שָׂדֶה וַתִּקָּחֵהוּ,
מִפְּרִי כַפֶּיהָ נָטְעָה כָּרֶם.
חָגְרָה בְעוֹז מָתְנֶיהָ,
וַתְּאַמֵּץ זְרוֹעֹתֶיהָ.
טָעֲמָה כִּי טוֹב סַחְרָהּ,
לֹא יִכְבֶּה בַלַּיְלָה נֵרָהּ.
יָדֶיהָ שִׁלְּחָה בַכִּישׁוֹר,
וְכַפֶּיהָ תָּמְכוּ פָלֶךְ.

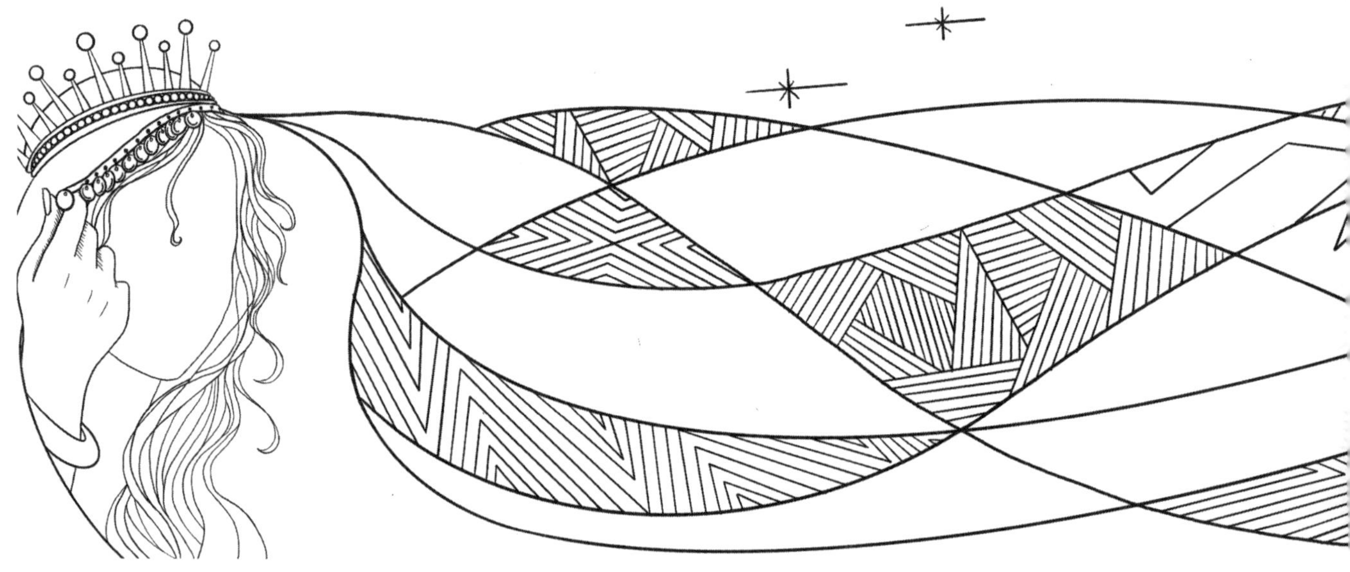

She extends her palm to the poor,
she reaches forth her hands [to help] the needy.
She does not fear for her household on account of the snow,
because her household is clothed in scarlet [wool].
She makes covers for herself,
her clothing is [made of valuable] linen and [the royal color of] purple.
Her husband is known at the gates,
[where] he sits with the elders of the land.
She makes linen cloth and sells it,
and delivers girdles to the Canaanite [merchant].
She is clothed in strength and splendor,
and she laughs at the last day.
She opens her mouth with wisdom,
and [words of] Torah kindness are upon her tongue.
She oversees the ways of her household,
and she never eats of the bread of laziness.
Her children stand and rejoice in her,
her husband, praises her.
Many daughters are valorous,
but you exceed them all!
Grace is a lie, and beauty is empty,
a woman who fears God, she should be praised.
Give her the fruit of her hands,
and let her works praise her at the gates!

Why do we sing *Eshet Chayil* on Friday night?

The origin of *Eshet Chayil* as a Shabbat evening song is unknown, but some suggest that the practice was instituted by kabbalists in the 17th century. It is now almost universally followed by observant Jewish communities worldwide. After a long week of toiling, it is appropriate to sing the praises of the Jewish wife and mother who traditionally has cared for her family, building and maintaining it through her loving attention to all aspects of the household and its members. While it is easy from our modern perch to see this song as archaic, and to criticize it for its singular focus on a married woman who is a mother working in a traditional homemaking setting, we should instead focus on the universal values that this song praises: love, attentiveness, industriousness, positivity, and inner strength over outer beauty.

כַּפָּהּ פָּרְשָׂה לֶעָנִי,
וְיָדֶיהָ שִׁלְּחָה לָאֶבְיוֹן.
לֹא תִירָא לְבֵיתָהּ מִשָּׁלֶג,
כִּי כָל בֵּיתָהּ לָבֻשׁ שָׁנִים.
מַרְבַדִּים עָשְׂתָה לָּהּ,
שֵׁשׁ וְאַרְגָּמָן לְבוּשָׁהּ.
נוֹדָע בַּשְּׁעָרִים בַּעְלָהּ,
בְּשִׁבְתּוֹ עִם זִקְנֵי אָרֶץ.
סָדִין עָשְׂתָה וַתִּמְכֹּר,
וַחֲגוֹר נָתְנָה לַכְּנַעֲנִי.
עֹז וְהָדָר לְבוּשָׁהּ,
וַתִּשְׂחַק לְיוֹם אַחֲרוֹן.
פִּיהָ פָּתְחָה בְחָכְמָה,
וְתוֹרַת חֶסֶד עַל לְשׁוֹנָהּ.
צוֹפִיָּה הֲלִיכוֹת בֵּיתָהּ,
וְלֶחֶם עַצְלוּת לֹא תֹאכֵל.
קָמוּ בָנֶיהָ וַיְאַשְּׁרוּהָ,
בַּעְלָהּ וַיְהַלְלָהּ.
רַבּוֹת בָּנוֹת עָשׂוּ חָיִל,
וְאַתְּ עָלִית עַל כֻּלָּנָה.
שֶׁקֶר הַחֵן וְהֶבֶל הַיֹּפִי,
אִשָּׁה יִרְאַת יְהֹוָה הִיא תִתְהַלָּל.
תְּנוּ לָהּ מִפְּרִי יָדֶיהָ,
וִיהַלְלוּהָ בַשְּׁעָרִים מַעֲשֶׂיהָ.

What is the meaning of *Eshet Chayil*?

On the simplest level, *Eshet Chayil* is a song that extols the praiseworthy characteristics of an idyllic Jewish woman. She is a wife upon whom her husband can rely and whose merits are increased by her good acts, who works industriously in a career, while also tending to the needs of her family and even her servants. The song comes from the last chapter of Proverbs, which is traditionally attributed to King Solomon. Proverbs is the quintessential Jewish example of "wisdom" literature, a genre of literature in ancient times in which authors distilled personal experience gathered over a lifetime into pithy expressions for dealing with life's mysteries and uncertainties and providing lessons on how to live a good life. Most of *Eshet Chayil* is of general applicability, but the end seems to call out a specific woman – "Many daughters are valorous, but you exceed them all!" To some commentators, this suggests that rather than being an ode to women generally, *Eshet Chayil* is an allegory for Shabbat, which is associated with the feminine aspect of God's nature – the *Shechinah*.

Blessing the Children

On Shabbat, continue here.

Traditionally, the father places his hands on the head of each child and recites the following blessing. Some have the custom of both parents giving the blessing. Many parents have the tradition to quietly share a private prayer or words with each child following the blessing.

For a boy begin by saying:

May God make you like Ephraim and Menashe.

For a girl begin by saying:

May God make you like Sarah, Rebecca, Rachel and Leah.

Conclude with the following blessing for both a boy and a girl:

May the Lord bless you and protect you.

May the Lord show you favor and be gracious to you.

May the Lord turn His face to you and grant you peace.

---

however, had no rivalry. Jacob recognized this special quality between them and, as if to demonstrate this, he blessed Ephraim, the younger, before Menashe, the older. King David rightly praised the blessing of peace among brothers in the 133rd psalm: "How good and pleasant is it for brothers to sit peacefully together!"

What is the connection between the Priestly Blessing and the Exodus?

As we will learn from the *Haggadah*, the Israelites remained "distinct" in Egypt. Joseph's two son, Ephraim and Menashe, more than any represent the resiliency of Jewish identity. They were the first Jewish children to be born outside the land of Israel. In the Holy Land, surrounded and supported by family and familiar customs, it is comparatively easy to maintain and strengthen a Jewish identity, but outside, doing so is exceedingly difficult. As Rabbi Samson Raphael Hirsch, the intellectual founder of the German orthodox movement, Derech Eretz, noted, despite being raised in an immoral Egypt, Ephraim and Menashe remained steadfast in their Jewish identities. If the *seder* falls on erev Shabbat, how appropriate that on the night when we celebrate, among other things, the continuity of the Jewish people, that we should bless our sons in the merit of Ephraim and Menashe, who exemplify a strong Jewish identity!

ברכת הבנים

On שבת, continue here.

Traditionally, the father places his hands on the head of each child and recites the following ברכה. Some have the custom of both parents giving the ברכה. Many parents have the tradition to quietly share a private prayer or words with each child following the ברכה.

For a boy begin by saying:

יְשִׂמְךָ אֱלֹהִים כְּאֶפְרַיִם וְכִמְנַשֶּׁה.

For a girl begin by saying:

יְשִׂימֵךְ אֱלֹהִים כְּשָׂרָה, רִבְקָה, רָחֵל וְלֵאָה.

Conclude with the following blessing for both a boy and a girl:

יְבָרֶכְךָ יְהֹוָה וְיִשְׁמְרֶךָ.
יָאֵר יְהֹוָה פָּנָיו אֵלֶיךָ וִיחֻנֶּךָּ.
יִשָּׂא יְהֹוָה פָּנָיו אֵלֶיךָ וְיָשֵׂם לְךָ שָׁלוֹם.

Q&A

What is the source of this blessing?

The main part of the blessing comes from the book of Numbers, chapter 6, in which God commands Moses to instruct his brother Aaron in the manner of blessing the Israelites. The priests are called upon to recite this blessing, and in so doing, God will bestow His blessing upon the Israelites. It is therefore called the "Priestly Blessing". It is undoubtedly one of the most beloved passages of the entire Torah as evidenced by various archeological finds. For example, in 1979, a dig at Jerusalem's City of David unearthed a 4 cm silver case containing a tiny scroll with the Priestly Blessing written upon it. Although other artifacts have been found with the Priestly Blessing, none have matched this find in terms of age. Dated to the 7th century BCE, prior to the destruction of the First Temple, it is more than 400 years older than the oldest Dead Sea Scroll.

Why do we pray that boys be like "Ephraim and Menashe"; not like the patriarchs?

While we ask God to make the girls like the matriarchs, we do not ask Him to make the sons like the patriarchs. One explanation for this is that Ephraim and Menashe were the first generation of Israelite siblings who did not quarrel. The relationships between Isaac and Yishmael, and Jacob and Esau, and among Jacob's children were all fraught with conflict. At the root of these arguments was primogeniture, the law that the firstborn inherits a double portion or a special blessing or role. Ephraim and Menashe,

KADESH

BLESS THE FIRST CUP

Kiddush for Passover Evening

The first cup of wine is poured, preferably by another person. The leader of the seder recites Kiddush as everyone stands. If Shabbat and the seder coincide, the blessing is recited before Havdalah.

On Shabbat, begin here:

And there was evening and there was morning,
the sixth day.
And the heaven and the earth were finished, and all their host.
And on the seventh day God finished His work which He had done,
and He rested on the seventh day from all His work which He had done.
And God blessed the seventh day, and sanctified it,
because He rested on it from all of His work, which God created in doing.

On weekdays, begin here:

Please pay attention, my masters.
Blessed are You, Lord, our God, King of the universe,
who creates the fruit of the vine.

On Shabbat, include words in parenthesis:

Blessed are You, Lord, our God, King of the universe,
who has chosen us from all peoples
and has raised us above all tongues and has sanctified us with His commandments.
And You have given us, Lord, our God, (Sabbaths for rest),
appointed times for happiness, holidays, and special times for joy,
(this Sabbath day, and) this Festival of Matzot,
our season of freedom (in love)
a holy convocation in memory of the Exodus from Egypt.
For You have chosen and sanctified us above all peoples,
Your (Sabbath, and) holy festivals (in love and favor)
You have given us as our heritage, for happiness and joy.
Blessed are You, Lord,
who sanctifies (the Sabbath and,) Israel, and the [appointed] times.

קדש

קידוש ליל הפסח

The first cup of wine is poured, preferably by another person. The leader of the סדר recites קידוש as everyone stands. If שבת and the סדר coincide, the ברכה is recited before הבדלה.

On שבת, begin here:

וַיְהִי עֶרֶב וַיְהִי בֹקֶר,
יוֹם הַשִּׁשִּׁי.
וַיְכֻלּוּ הַשָּׁמַיִם וְהָאָרֶץ וְכָל צְבָאָם.
וַיְכַל אֱלֹהִים בַּיּוֹם הַשְּׁבִיעִי מְלַאכְתּוֹ אֲשֶׁר עָשָׂה,
וַיִּשְׁבֹּת בַּיּוֹם הַשְּׁבִיעִי מִכָּל מְלַאכְתּוֹ אֲשֶׁר עָשָׂה.
וַיְבָרֶךְ אֱלֹהִים אֶת יוֹם הַשְּׁבִיעִי וַיְקַדֵּשׁ אוֹתוֹ,
כִּי בוֹ שָׁבַת מִכָּל מְלַאכְתּוֹ אֲשֶׁר בָּרָא אֱלֹהִים לַעֲשׂוֹת.

On weekdays, begin here:

סַבְרִי מָרָנָן.
בָּרוּךְ אַתָּה יְהֹוָה אֱלֹהֵינוּ מֶלֶךְ הָעוֹלָם,
בּוֹרֵא פְּרִי הַגָּפֶן.

On שבת, include words in parenthesis:

בָּרוּךְ אַתָּה יְהֹוָה אֱלֹהֵינוּ מֶלֶךְ הָעוֹלָם,
אֲשֶׁר בָּחַר בָּנוּ מִכָּל עָם
וְרוֹמְמָנוּ מִכָּל לָשׁוֹן וְקִדְּשָׁנוּ בְּמִצְוֹתָיו.
וַתִּתֶּן לָנוּ יְהֹוָה אֱלֹהֵינוּ בְּאַהֲבָה (שַׁבָּתוֹת לִמְנוּחָה וּ)
מוֹעֲדִים לְשִׂמְחָה, חַגִּים וּזְמַנִּים לְשָׂשׂוֹן,
אֶת יוֹם (הַשַּׁבָּת הַזֶּה וְאֶת יוֹם) חַג הַמַּצּוֹת הַזֶּה,
זְמַן חֵרוּתֵנוּ (בְּאַהֲבָה),
מִקְרָא קֹדֶשׁ, זֵכֶר לִיצִיאַת מִצְרָיִם.
כִּי בָנוּ בָחַרְתָּ וְאוֹתָנוּ קִדַּשְׁתָּ מִכָּל הָעַמִּים,
(וְשַׁבָּת) וּמוֹעֲדֵי קָדְשֶׁךָ (בְּאַהֲבָה וּבְרָצוֹן),
בְּשִׂמְחָה וּבְשָׂשׂוֹן הִנְחַלְתָּנוּ.
בָּרוּךְ אַתָּה יְהֹוָה,
מְקַדֵּשׁ (הַשַּׁבָּת וְ) יִשְׂרָאֵל וְהַזְּמַנִּים.

On Saturday night add the following two paragraphs:

Blessed are You, Lord, our God, King of the universe,
who creates the light of the fire.

Hold up the fingers to the candle flame to see the light reflected upon the nails. Then continue with:

Blessed are You, Lord, our God, King of the universe,
who distinguishes between the holy and the profane,
between light and darkness, between Israel and the nations,
between the seventh day and the six working days.
Between the holiness of the Sabbath
and the holiness of the Festival you have distinguished,
and You have sanctified the seventh day above the six working days.
You distinguished and sanctified Your people Israel with Your holiness.
Blessed are You, Lord, who distinguishes between the holy and the holy.

On all days continue here:

**Blessed are You, Lord, our God, King of the universe,
who has granted us life and sustenance and permitted us to reach this [special] time.**

Drink while reclining to the left and do not recite a blessing after drinking.

What else do the four cups of wine represent?

The four cups also correspond to the four special foods of the *seder*: *matzah*, Passover offering, *maror* and *charoset*. Another explanation is that the four cups hint at the four nations that oppressed the Israelites in ancient times: Egypt, Assyria, Babylon, and Rome.

What other things happen in groups of four during the *seder*?

In addition to the Four Cups, there are also the Four Questions and the Four Sons, as well as less obviously, four pieces of *matzah* (the original three, of which one is broken into two, making four pieces).

How do Jewish women relate to the number four?

There are four matriarchs of the Jewish people: Sarah, Rebecca, Rachel, and Leah. The Maharal of Prague explained that the four cups also correspond to these four matriarchs.

Why is this *Kiddush* different than any other *Kiddush*?

At every Shabbat *Kiddush* we explicitly recognize God's providence in taking the Jewish people out of Egypt. As slaves in Egypt, there was never a day of rest. Because of God's redemption of the Jewish people from slavery, we are free people who can, and indeed should rest on the Sabbath. How much more powerful is the message of this *Kiddush* on the very holiday that commemorates the Exodus itself!

On מוצאי שבת add the following two paragraphs:

בָּרוּךְ אַתָּה יְהֹוָה אֱלֹהֵינוּ מֶלֶךְ הָעוֹלָם,
בּוֹרֵא מְאוֹרֵי הָאֵשׁ.

Hold up the fingers to the candle flame to see the light reflected upon the nails. Then continue with:

בָּרוּךְ אַתָּה יְהֹוָה אֱלֹהֵינוּ מֶלֶךְ הָעוֹלָם,
הַמַּבְדִּיל בֵּין קֹדֶשׁ לְחֹל,
בֵּין אוֹר לְחֹשֶׁךְ, בֵּין יִשְׂרָאֵל לָעַמִּים,
בֵּין יוֹם הַשְּׁבִיעִי לְשֵׁשֶׁת יְמֵי הַמַּעֲשֶׂה.
בֵּין קְדֻשַּׁת שַׁבָּת
לִקְדֻשַּׁת יוֹם טוֹב הִבְדַּלְתָּ,
וְאֶת יוֹם הַשְּׁבִיעִי מִשֵּׁשֶׁת יְמֵי הַמַּעֲשֶׂה קִדַּשְׁתָּ.
הִבְדַּלְתָּ וְקִדַּשְׁתָּ אֶת עַמְּךָ יִשְׂרָאֵל בִּקְדֻשָּׁתֶךָ.
בָּרוּךְ אַתָּה יְהֹוָה הַמַּבְדִּיל בֵּין קֹדֶשׁ לְקֹדֶשׁ.

On all days continue here:

בָּרוּךְ אַתָּה יְהֹוָה אֱלֹהֵינוּ מֶלֶךְ הָעוֹלָם,
שֶׁהֶחֱיָנוּ וְקִיְּמָנוּ וְהִגִּיעָנוּ לַזְּמַן הַזֶּה.

Drink while reclining to the left and do not recite a ברכה after drinking.

What is the meaning or purpose of *Kiddush*?

The *Kiddush* is a formal consecration of the holiness of the Sabbath and festivals. On Shabbat we recognize that the universe was not created by chance, but rather God created it. Just as He rested on the seventh day, we rest on the seventh day to make it holy. So too the festivals are holy, and we rest on them as well. The *Kiddush* is meant to mark this event as something special and holy.

Why must the timing of *Kiddush* not be delayed?

While the *Kiddush* done on Shabbat and any *Yom Tov* is Rabbinic in origin and can be delayed, the *Kiddush* of *Pesach* cannot be delayed. It must be done as soon as possible. The reason given by the Baal HaTanya is for the *seder* to begin as soon as possible. We should begin the *seder* as soon as possible so that, as the *Shulchan Aruch* states, we can begin to eat for the sake of the children. Even from the very beginning of the *seder* we learn of the centrality of children to the event. We want them to participate and to ask questions. However, if we delay too long, our sages understood that overly-hungry children would not be able to concentrate.

Why do we drink four cups of wine?

The traditional explanation for why we drink four cups of wine is that the four cups correspond to the four expressions of God's salvation for the Jewish people. As it is said, "And I will bring you out, and I will redeem you, and I will save you, and I will take you."

URCHATZ
HANDWASH WITHOUT BLESSING

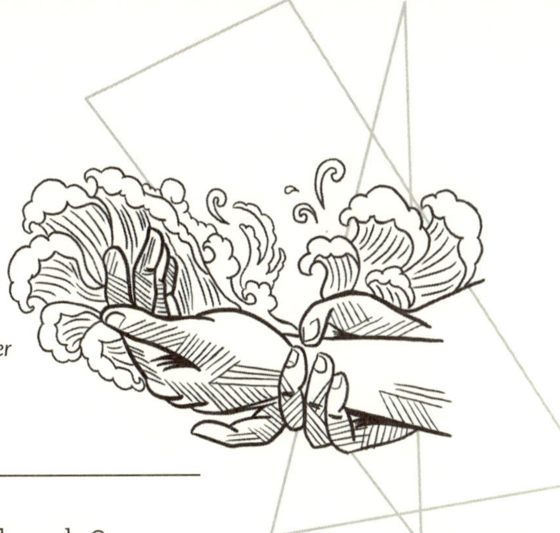

Wash your hands, but do not say a blessing. It is preferable that a pitcher of water should be used and a bowl. It is also preferable that another person ritually pours water over another's hands, rather than each person washing his or her own hands.

Why do we not say a blessing when we wash our hands?

Although there is a general commandment to wash hands before eating any food dipped in liquid, there is a dispute as to whether this commandment only relates to times when there is a Temple. In deference to this minority view, we wash but do not say a blessing, in case we are not obligated, in which case we would be saying God's name in vain.

KARPAS
DIP THE GREEN VEGETABLE

Take a vegetable and dip less than a k'zayit into salt water.
As you dip, say the following blessing:

Blessed are You, Lord, our God, King of the universe,

who creates the fruit of the earth.

As it still a long way until the festive meal begins, it has become common to dip a variety of food items in a variety of dips.
Make sure to say the appropriate blessing.
Eat enough so that you can concentrate without being distracted by thoughts of the upcoming meal, but not so much that you become full.

What does the *karpas* represent?

There are many things the *karpas* may represent, but a powerful image for *Chag HaAviv*, the Festival of Spring, is surely the green that accompanies the world each spring season as the ground renews itself, thus symbolizing the season in which Passover is celebrated.

ורחץ

Wash your hands, but do not say a ברכה. It is preferable that a pitcher of water should be used and a bowl. It is also preferable that another person ritually pours water over another's hands, rather than each person washing his or her own hands.

Why do we wash our hands before eating the Karpas?

Although we wash our hands before eating the *karpas*, there is a general commandment in the Talmud to wash before eating any food dipped in a water and certain other liquids. Although we do not follow this throughout the year, because of the importance of Passover, we honor this commandment at the *seder*. As with many of the unusual practices of the *seder*, we also hope that doing so sparks questions and discussion among children.

כרפס

Take a vegetable and dip less than a כזית into salt water.
As you dip, say the following ברכה:

בָּרוּךְ אַתָּה יְהוָה אֱלֹהֵינוּ מֶלֶךְ הָעוֹלָם,
בּוֹרֵא פְּרִי הָאֲדָמָה.

As it still a long way until the festive meal begins, it has become common to dip a variety of food items in a variety of dips. Make sure to say the appropriate ברכה. Eat enough so that you can concentrate without being distracted by thoughts of the upcoming meal, but not so much that you become full.

Q&A

Where does the word "*karpas*" come from? What does it mean?

The word "*karpas*" is not Hebrew. It may come from the Greek word, *karpos*, meaning "fruit" or "produce". This part of the *seder* appears to have its roots in the Greek symposium, from which some of the *seder* traditions originate. The Greeks would dip appetizers in salt water or other dips during the discussion or debates of the symposium.

Why do we dip in salt water?

It's generally the view that we dip in salt water because it symbolizes the tears of the enslaved Israelites in Egypt. Rabbi Lord Jonathan Sacks relates another beautiful metaphor. The *karpas* may be sweet, but dipping it in salt makes it become sour. This reminds us that freedom, though sweet, becomes sour when we use it to mistreat others.

How much is a "*k'zayit*"?

A *k'zayit* is about the size of an olive – the smallest ritually acceptable amount to avoid having to say a blessing before eating it.

YACHATZ

BREAK THE MIDDLE MATZAH

The leader breaks the middle matzah in two, leaving the smaller half and concealing the larger piece for use after the festive meal as the Afikoman.

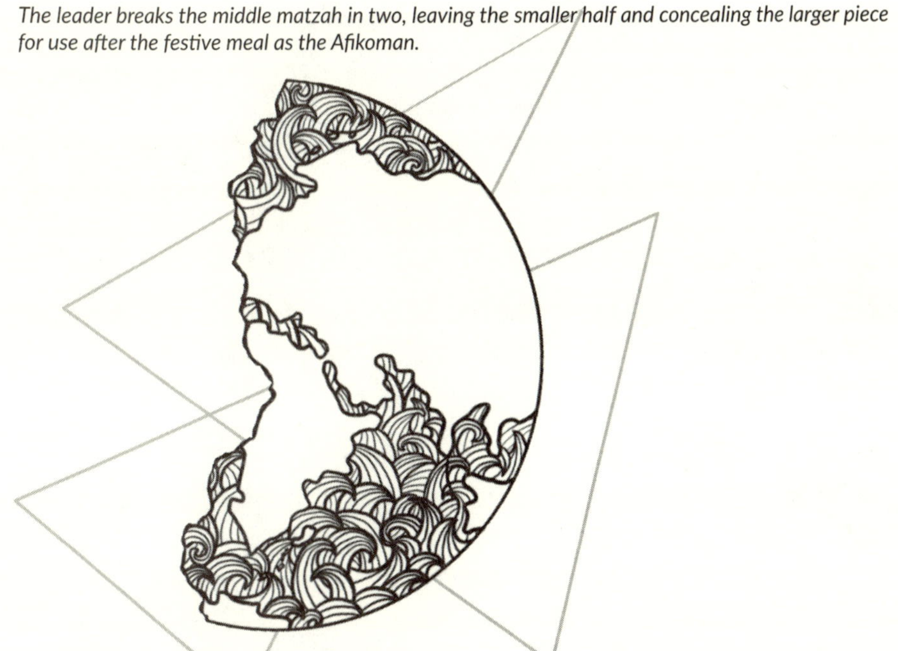

---

reason is that following the destruction of the Temple, *matzah* took the place of the Passover offering. Just as the Passover offering was eaten at the end of the Passover meal, to emphasize that it was holy, rather than something needed to satisfy hunger, so too part of the *matzah* is reserved for after the festive meal is over.

What else does the "broken" *matzah* represent?

The broken *matzah* reminds us that the world itself is broken. There is still oppression and slavery. The world can only be made whole when we find the other half, symbolized by the *Afikoman*. The *seder* is a microcosm of the Jewish people's journey that starts off in Egypt in slavery, but ends in freedom.

Why do we dip at all?

While the tradition of dipping the *karpas* in salt water may have Greek origins, our Rabbis teach that the dipping is meant to cause the children at the table to ask questions. Another lesser-known interpretation is that dipping the *karpas* in salt water evokes the memory of Joseph's colorful coat dipped in blood by his brothers. Another act of dipping related to the story of Exodus is when the Israelites took bunches of hyssop and dipped them in the blood of the Passover offering, using it to spread the blood on the doorposts to protect themselves from the killing of the firstborn.

The leader breaks the middle מצה *in two, leaving the smaller half and concealing the larger piece for use after the festive meal as the* אפיקומן.

Why are there three Matzot?

Of the three *matzot*, the upper and lower represent the double portion of manna that fell before the Sabbaths and festivals when the Israelites wandered in the wilderness after the Exodus. The third *matzah* represents the special duty to eat unleavened bread on Passover.

Why do we break the middle *matzah*?

There are two reasons we break the middle *matzah*. The first is that, as the "bread of oppression" or the "bread of the poor person", it reminds us of those who do not have enough. They must literally break their bread in two, saving part because they cannot be sure they will have food to eat later. The second

MAGID

TELL THE STORY OF THE EXODUS

Hold up the seder plate and display the middle matzah while saying the following paragraph.

For a transliteration of the Hebrew text, please turn to page 168.

This is the bread of oppression

our ancestors ate in the land of Egypt.

Let all who are hungry come and eat,

let all who are in need come and join us.

Now we are here; next year in the land of Israel.

Now we are slaves;

next year we shall be free.

Put down the seder plate and cover the matzah.

How is it appropriate to invite the poor to eat such an unpleasant food?

While it may seem odd to invite those who are hungry to eat a bread of suffering, there is a profound message here. Just as *matzah* was the bread eaten by slaves, it also was the food that they ate as they left Egypt. It is this invitation to share with others that transforms oppression into liberty. When people are slaves, or when they are oppressed, they fear for tomorrow and may feel unable to share. Sharing is an act of a free person.

What is the meaning of this opening passage?

One of the reasons for Jewish resiliency and continuity is the understanding of our past. Much of the *seder* relates to the past – the time leading up to Egypt, the slavery in Egypt and the Exodus from Egypt. Remembering the past, and the fact that God delivered us from Egypt, helps us have faith that God will deliver us again in the future.

What other important messages might this passage be teaching?

The invitation also serves to remind us that there are people in the community and the world who are oppressed. This passage is a call to action. It is not enough just to recognize there are people who do not have enough to eat. We also need to be compassionate for their condition and then act to do something to help them.

מגיד

Hold up the seder plate and display the middle מצה while saying the following paragraph.

For a transliteration of the following text, please turn to page 168.

הָא לַחְמָא עַנְיָא

דִּי אֲכַלוּ אַבְהָתָנָא בְּאַרְעָא דְמִצְרָיִם.
כָּל דִּכְפִין יֵיתֵי וְיֵיכֹל,
כָּל דִּצְרִיךְ יֵיתֵי וְיִפְסַח.
הָשַׁתָּא הָכָא, לְשָׁנָה הַבָּאָה בְּאַרְעָא דְיִשְׂרָאֵל.
הָשַׁתָּא עַבְדֵי,
לְשָׁנָה הַבָּאָה בְּנֵי חוֹרִין.

Put down the seder plate and cover the מצה.

Q&A

Why is the opening paragraph in Aramaic, instead of Hebrew?

The *Haggadah* was composed over many centuries. Aramaic was the language spoken in Israel before the destruction of the Second Temple. Generally, it was acceptable to use the spoken language for prayer if Hebrew was not understood. This suggests that this section of the *Haggadah* was added in the late second Temple Period when most Jews spoke and understood Aramaic as their first language.

Why is *matzah* called the bread of oppression?

Although the most common reason for eating *matzah* is to remind us of the haste with which the Israelites fled Egypt – as their bread did not have time to rise – *matzah* was also a food that was eaten by slaves. Therefore, *matzah* further reminds us of the food our ancestors ate during slavery and the suffering of their lives. In addition, this opening line of the *Magid* sets up a journey of sorts. It begins with *matzah* as the bread of oppression, but over the course of the evening it is transformed and ultimately the *seder* ends with eating the *Afikoman*, which represents the bread of freedom.

The Four Questions

Pour the second cup of wine.
Customs differ regarding the recitation of the Four Questions.
Traditionally, the youngest child capable of doing so should sing them.
However, today all children below the age of bar/bat mitzvah may do so.

For a transliteration of the Hebrew text, please turn to page 168.

What makes this night different from all other nights?

On all other nights, we eat [either] bread or Matzah,
[but] tonight [we eat] only Matzah.

On all other nights, we eat many different greens,
[but] tonight [we eat] bitter herbs.

On all other nights, we do not dip [our food] at all,
[but] tonight [we dip] twice.

On all other nights, we eat sitting or reclining,
[but] tonight we all recline.

What is the source of the Four Questions?

We have just interrupted the Magid by pouring the second cup, which we will not bless and drink until just before Shulchan Orech. This is an unusual change to the normal practice, which Rashi suggests is meant to stimulate questions by the son. But what if the son is not mature enough to notice this change and ask about it? The Mishna relates in tractate Pesachim (10:4) that if the son is not mature enough to ask about this (literally, lacks the "knowledge"), then the father is obligated to teach the son by asking "why is this night different from all other nights?" The Mishna then offers four answers to this question. Those four answers are the basis for the Four Questions, which have become part of the Haggadah in its present form.

Why does the fourth answer concern reclining, and what does that teach us?

The Mishna in tractate Pesachim (10:4) offers four answers to the question of "why is this night different from all other nights?" Three of these answers are included in the Haggadah, but the fourth, is not. The one answer that is not included is that on all other nights we eat roasted, stewed or cooked meat, "but tonight, [we eat] the roasted meat [of the Passover offering]." In its place, the sages included an alternative, "on all other nights, we eat sitting or reclining, [but] tonight we all recline." The most obvious reason that the answer concerning eating the Passover offering is replaced is that in the post–Temple period, where the sacrificial system has ended, we cannot eat the Passover offering. But why is it replaced with an answer concerning reclining? Reclining is a distinct characteristic of the seder, which the sages mandated even "the poorest of Jews" should take part in. As evidenced from multiple Talmudic tractates, as well as archeological finds, reclining while eating was a regular practice among

מה נשתנה

Pour the second cup of wine.
Customs differ regarding the recitation of the מה נשתנה.
Traditionally, the youngest child capable of doing so should sing them.
However, today all children below the age of bar/bat mitzvah may do so.

For a transliteration of the following text, please turn to page 168.

מַה נִּשְׁתַּנָּה הַלַּיְלָה הַזֶּה מִכָּל הַלֵּילוֹת?

שֶׁבְּכָל הַלֵּילוֹת אָנוּ אוֹכְלִין חָמֵץ וּמַצָּה,
הַלַּיְלָה הַזֶּה כֻּלּוֹ מַצָּה.

שֶׁבְּכָל הַלֵּילוֹת אָנוּ אוֹכְלִין שְׁאָר יְרָקוֹת,
הַלַּיְלָה הַזֶּה מָרוֹר.

שֶׁבְּכָל הַלֵּילוֹת אֵין אָנוּ מַטְבִּילִין אֲפִילוּ פַּעַם אֶחָת,
הַלַּיְלָה הַזֶּה שְׁתֵּי פְעָמִים.

שֶׁבְּכָל הַלֵּילוֹת אָנוּ אוֹכְלִין בֵּין יוֹשְׁבִין וּבֵין מְסֻבִּין,
הַלַּיְלָה הַזֶּה כֻּלָּנוּ מְסֻבִּין.

Q&A

Why do we ask questions at the *seder*?

The Torah states regarding Passover, "And if your children should ask you, 'What is this service to you?', You shall say ..." This is the source of our obligation to answer questions during Passover. On a deeper level, children do not learn simply by listening. Rather children – and even adults – learn best by asking questions. Asking questions is a core part of being Jewish, and a great difference between Judaism and other religions. Other religions had founders who received a philosophy, morality, or religious practice, which they then passed on. This requires great faith, because how can anyone know that the founder really received any teaching at all? As a result, questioning can be seen as a sign of a lack of faith. Islam, for example, literally means "submission", implying that faith requires relinquishing questioning. Similarly, the third century Christian philosopher, Tirtullian, once said "I believe it because it is absurd", a maxim suggesting faith need not be based in reason. "Israel" in contrast means "to struggle with God". Jews are meant to struggle, to challenge and to ask questions. Abraham challenged God (in response to God's declaration of destroying Sodom and Gomorrah, Abraham asked, "Will the Judge of the earth not perform justice?"), Moses challenged God (by saying "Why have you brought trouble upon this people?"), and many of our prophets also challenged God (Jeremiah asked, "Why do the wicked prosper?"). For Jews, questioning is the path to learning and to a strengthening of faith.

Why are these not called the Four Answers?

While this section of the Haggadah has come to be known in English as the Four Questions, in Hebrew they are known simply as the Mah Nishtanah, which means "how [or why] is [this night] different". In Hebrew, the Mah Nishtanah is clearly a single question with four answers, but even in English, the Four Questions are rarely translated as four distinct questions.

How do the Four Questions relate to the Four Sons?

The Four Questions correspond to the Four Sons. The Wise Son asks the first question, which is a profound question about the central symbol of the *seder*, the *matzah*. The Wicked Son asks about the *maror*, because the *maror* is bitter, and the Wicked Son tastes only the bitterness of Jewish life, not its sweetness. The Simple Son asks about dipping, because the dipping is meant to provoke the questioning of even a small child. And the Son Who Does Not Know How to Ask, asks about reclining, which is not even a question about part of the *seder* itself, but rather about people's behavior around the *seder* table.

Uncover the seder plate and the matzot.

We Were Slaves to Pharaoh in Egypt,
and the Lord, our God, brought us out of there
with a strong hand and an outstretched arm.
And if the Holy One, blessed is He, had not brought
our ancestors out of Egypt,
then we, and our children, and our children's children,
would still be enslaved to Pharaoh in Egypt.
And even were we all wise, all intelligent, all aged,
and knowledgeable in the Torah,
[still] the command would be upon us
to tell of the Exodus from Egypt.
And the more one tells of the Exodus from Egypt,
the more admirable it is.

Why do we say that had God not brought our ancestors out of Egypt then "we would still be enslaved"?

The reason we say that "we would still be enslaved" is because each person must see himself or herself as personally connected to the events of the Exodus. We are connecting ourselves directly to the past. This makes the Exodus a timeless event. Even more concretely, if the Jewish people had not been taken out, simply put, there would be no Jewish people. That is even worse than slavery!

Why would even the wisest Rabbi at a *seder* by himself, need to tell the story?

The point of the *seder* is not just to learn about the Exodus. We are not obligated to tell the story simply to know what happened. The point is for us to connect to the story. The story itself is timeless and offers many layers of meaning. Even if you tell the story every year, you can always learn something new from it.

the upper classes during the Second Temple period. One can infer then that it was not so outside the upper classes. The lower classes did not have the luxury of eating leisurely, while reclining on a couch. Reclining was seen by the sages as symbolic of free people, and therefore a potent symbol of the release from slavery, which they incorporated into the seder. We can also learn something about the origin of the custom of reclining. Reclining while eating was a common practice attested to in Greek literature, including Plato's Symposium. This is possibly another indication of the influence that Greek culture had not only on Judaic culture, but on the structure of the seder itself.

Uncover the seder plate and the מצות.

עֲבָדִים הָיִינוּ לְפַרְעֹה בְּמִצְרָיִם,
וַיּוֹצִיאֵנוּ יְהֹוָה אֱלֹהֵינוּ מִשָּׁם
בְּיָד חֲזָקָה וּבִזְרוֹעַ נְטוּיָה.
וְאִלּוּ לֹא הוֹצִיא הַקָּדוֹשׁ בָּרוּךְ הוּא
אֶת אֲבוֹתֵינוּ מִמִּצְרָיִם,
הֲרֵי אָנוּ וּבָנֵינוּ וּבְנֵי בָנֵינוּ
מְשֻׁעְבָּדִים הָיִינוּ לְפַרְעֹה בְּמִצְרָיִם.
וַאֲפִלּוּ כֻּלָּנוּ חֲכָמִים, כֻּלָּנוּ נְבוֹנִים, כֻּלָּנוּ זְקֵנִים,
כֻּלָּנוּ יוֹדְעִים אֶת הַתּוֹרָה,
מִצְוָה עָלֵינוּ
לְסַפֵּר בִּיצִיאַת מִצְרָיִם.
וְכָל הַמַּרְבֶּה לְסַפֵּר בִּיצִיאַת מִצְרַיִם,
הֲרֵי זֶה מְשֻׁבָּח.

Q&A

Why was this passage, "We were slaves", chosen to begin answering the four questions which preceded it?

The Mishnah states that the telling of the Exodus must "begin with the shame and end with the praise". There are two views on how to fulfill this obligation. The first view, given here, is from Shmuel, a great Babylonian rabbi of the 3rd century CE. Shmuel believed that the main theme of the *seder* is of the Jewish people's physical redemption ("we were slaves"). Therefore, we start the story with the shame of the physical slavery, and end with the physical freedom that occurred when God led the Jewish people out of Egypt. However, Shmuel's counterpart, Rav, held the view that the main theme of the *seder* is of the Jewish people's spiritual redemption. That is why later in the *Haggadah* we will read about our spiritual redemption.

Once, Rabbi Eliezer and Rabbi Yehoshua and Rabbi Elazar ben Azaria
and Rabbi Akiva and Rabbi Tarfon reclined [at a seder] in Bnei Brak,
and they told of the Exodus from Egypt all that night,
until their students came in and said to them:
"Teachers – the time for saying the Shema of the morning has arrived."

Rabbi Elazar ben Azaria said:
"I am like 70 years old,
and never have I merited to speak of the Exodus from Egypt at night,
until Ben Zoma interpreted.
As it is said,
"So that you remember the day of your Exodus from Egypt
all the days of your life."
"The days of your life" [mean] in the days.
"All the days of your life" [includes] the nights.
But the sages say:
"The days of your life" [would only mean in] this world.
"All the days of your life" brings in the time of the Messiah.

---

important figures in creating Rabbinic Judaism following the loss of the Temple, and in keeping the Jewish people together in the face of so much tragedy. Despite all the tragedy of that era, they still carried on with their *seder*. This story teaches us about the resiliency of Judaism and should give us hope that despite any tragedy, we can move forward.

Why does Rabbi Elazar ben Azaria say he is "like" 70 years old?

Rabbi Elazar ben Azaria was one of the great *tannaim* (leading rabbis of the Mishnaic period), a *kohen* of aristocratic birth and of great wealth. The Talmud records that he was appointed the *nasi*, or prince, who acted as the de facto political leader of the Jewish community following the destruction of the Second Temple, at the age of 18. It could be that this statement by him was made while he was still young. In exclaiming that he was "like 70 years old", he might have been saying that despite his youth, he was nevertheless wise. There is a tale that grew up around this view, which stated that when Rabbi Elazar was appointed *nasi*, his beard turned white. A less fanciful, and more straightforward reading based on another passage in the Jerusalem Talmud is that he was already 68 when he made this statement. Therefore it could be translated as "almost 70", rather than "like 70". As the Psalmist stated in psalm 90, "the days of our lives are 70 years". So Rabbi Elazar was simply saying he had lived a full life.

מַעֲשֶׂה בְּרַבִּי אֱלִיעֶזֶר וְרַבִּי יְהוֹשֻׁעַ וְרַבִּי אֶלְעָזָר בֶּן עֲזַרְיָה
וְרַבִּי עֲקִיבָא וְרַבִּי טַרְפוֹן שֶׁהָיוּ מְסֻבִּין בִּבְנֵי בְרַק,
וְהָיוּ מְסַפְּרִים בִּיצִיאַת מִצְרַיִם כָּל אוֹתוֹ הַלַּיְלָה
עַד שֶׁבָּאוּ תַלְמִידֵיהֶם וְאָמְרוּ לָהֶם:
רַבּוֹתֵינוּ, הִגִּיעַ זְמַן קְרִיאַת שְׁמַע שֶׁל שַׁחֲרִית.

אָמַר רַבִּי אֶלְעָזָר בֶּן עֲזַרְיָה:
הֲרֵי אֲנִי כְּבֶן שִׁבְעִים שָׁנָה,
וְלֹא זָכִיתִי שֶׁתֵּאָמֵר יְצִיאַת מִצְרַיִם בַּלֵּילוֹת
עַד שֶׁדְּרָשָׁהּ בֶּן זוֹמָא.
שֶׁנֶּאֱמַר:
לְמַעַן תִּזְכֹּר אֶת יוֹם צֵאתְךָ מֵאֶרֶץ מִצְרַיִם
כֹּל יְמֵי חַיֶּיךָ.
יְמֵי חַיֶּיךָ– הַיָּמִים,
כֹּל יְמֵי חַיֶּיךָ– הַלֵּילוֹת.
וַחֲכָמִים אוֹמְרִים:
יְמֵי חַיֶּיךָ– הָעוֹלָם הַזֶּה,
כֹּל יְמֵי חַיֶּיךָ– לְהָבִיא לִימוֹת הַמָּשִׁיחַ.

Why does this story of the five Rabbis follow the section *Avadim Hayinu*?

We have just learned that everyone has a duty to tell the story of the Exodus from Egypt, even if old and wise. The *Haggadah* therefore follows immediately with an example of five great Rabbis at a *seder*. They clearly knew the story well, and even demonstrated that despite their years, they were still capable of learning new things. This section also demonstrates to us how we should conduct our *seder*. These rabbis spent the entire night in discussion, even until the time for saying the *Shema* in the morning had arrived. While we may not be able to devote such energy and time as these great Rabbis, we should nevertheless tell the story, ask and answer questions, and continue to learn from others and from the story itself.

What can we learn from the fact that the *Haggadah* is relating a story about a *seder* held at that place (Bnei Brak) and time?

These five Rabbis lived during the incredibly turbulent times following the destruction of the Second Temple. Rabbi Akiva was the principal Rabbinic supporter of Bar Kochba, who led a rebellion against Roman rule in 130 CE, which briefly led to Jewish autonomy for several years. These Rabbis were

The Four Sons

Blessed is the Omnipresent,

blessed is He.

Blessed is the One who gave the Torah to his people, Israel,

blessed is He.

"May *HaMakom* [the "Omnipresent"] comfort you among the other mourners of Zion and Jerusalem". This appellation, or identifying name for God, conveys the idea that although in times of trouble He appears absent, He never is. This is consistent with Rabban Gamliel's view of the transcendent God who is nevertheless imminently present. Using the name, *HaMakom*, reaffirms our faith that we are never alone because God is always together with us, an idea that is especially important when we are bereaved in a "place" of sadness.

Why does the *Haggadah* introduce the Four Sons, which are a response to the Four Questions, with a blessing of "HaMakom"?

As Rabbi Shimon Schwab suggests, in introducing the section of the four sons, the *Haggadah* is explicitly offering comfort to those present who have no children. Such people have neither heard their own children ask the Four Questions, nor are they obligated on the *mitzvah* to "tell [וְהִגַּדְתָּ] your child that day". This opening blessing may also be seen as comfort for parents who have children, but whose children are wicked, or simple, or do not know how to ask questions. Parents can take faith that God is with them in this "place" too. The Torah provides answers for any person dealing with any situation.

The Torah speaks of four types of sons:

One who is wise,

and one who is wicked,

and one who is simple,

and one who does not know how to ask.

---

child, 'We were slaves to Pharaoh in Egypt and God brought us out of Egypt with a strong hand.'" Our Rabbis saw that each passage was a distinct type of instruction that relates to the personalities of four distinct types of children.

What are other meanings of the Four Sons?

Each child can also be seen as representing a different type of Jew. The Wise Son represents the Jew who is engaged and wants to learn. The Wicked Son represents the Jew who asks not because he wants to learn, but because he wants to dismiss. The Simple Son represents the Jew who lacks an

ארבעת הבנים

בָּרוּךְ הַמָּקוֹם,
בָּרוּךְ הוּא.
בָּרוּךְ שֶׁנָּתַן תּוֹרָה לְעַמּוֹ יִשְׂרָאֵל,
בָּרוּךְ הוּא.

Q&A

What does "*HaMakom*" mean?

The Hebrew word, "*HaMakom*", literally means "the Place". It is commonly translated as "Omnipresent", meaning, present at all places and at all times. In the *midrash*, "*HaMakom*" means "He is the Place of the world, and the world is not His place". This suggests that the world exists only within God, but God is not of the world – He exists independently of it. Rabban Gamliel, one of the great rabbis who lived following the destruction of the second Temple, conceptualized God as existing not outside of our universe, but as the space in which the universe itself exists. In this view, "*HaMakom*" can be seen to mean "All-Encompassing One". This may seem like God is distant, or that His transcendence means we cannot come close to Him. Jewish monotheism was a stark refutation of the paganism of the ancient world, where the gods were seen as intimately part of nature itself. Yes, God is far away from the material world, but in Rabban Gamliel's vision, He is also intimately close. God is not out of reach, because the world, and everything in it, including Mankind, is part of His ubiquitous presence.

When else do we use the name "*HaMakom*" when referring to God?

The name *HaMakom* is often used at times of sadness. For example, when greeting a mourner, traditionally one says, "*HaMakom yenachem etchem b'toch sha'ar aveiley tzion v'yerushalayim*", meaning

---

כְּנֶגֶד אַרְבָּעָה בָנִים דִּבְּרָה תוֹרָה:
אֶחָד חָכָם,
וְאֶחָד רָשָׁע,
וְאֶחָד תָּם,
וְאֶחָד שֶׁאֵינוֹ יוֹדֵעַ לִשְׁאֹל.

Q&A

What is the source in the Torah for the Four Sons?

Four passages in the Torah relate how a parent should teach children about the Exodus from Egypt. The first is "And if your children should ask you, 'What is this rite you perform?' you should say, 'It is a *Pesach* [Passover offering] of God, for He passed over the houses of the children of Israel in Egypt while He struck the Egyptians, but saved those in our houses.'" The second is, "And you shall tell your child on that day, 'It is because of what God did for me when I went out of Egypt.'" The third is "If in that time your child should ask you, 'What is this?' You shall say to him, 'With a strong hand God brought us out of Egypt, from the house of slavery.'" And the fourth is "When, in times to come, your children ask you, 'What are the testimonies, statutes, and laws that God our God commanded you?' you shall say to your

What other types of sons can you think of?

Rabbi Menachem Mendel Schneerson, the last Rebbe of Chabad, spoke of a fifth son – the son who is not even at the *seder*. The Rebbe recognized that as a result of assimilation, generations of Jews have been born who have no interest in Judaism or have no knowledge of Passover and the *seder* itself. They are not represented by any of the Four Sons of the *Haggadah*. They stand completely outside Judaism altogether. Rabbi Schneerson challenged us to exert effort to engage with these disconnected Jews with *ahavat Yisrael* (love for a fellow Jew) in order to bring them back to Judaism and into the community of the Four Sons. The ultimate goal is to elevate them into a "wise" son.

The Wise Son, what does he say?

"What are the testimonies, the statutes, and the laws

that the Lord, our God, commanded you?"

And you must tell him the laws of Passover:

"They may not conclude after the Pesach [Passover offering] with an *Afikoman*."

What can we learn from the fact that the passage of the Wise Son comes from the book of Deuteronomy, while the other three come from the book of Exodus?

Wisdom is not the same as knowledge. Wisdom is knowledge gained over time. The Wise Son's question demonstrates wisdom because it comes from the book of Deuteronomy. The events in Deuteronomy occurred 40 years after the Exodus. The Wise Son's question suggests that to best understand the significance of the Exodus takes time. It is difficult to understand an event when it is happening. Only with the passage of time does one gain the wisdom to truly understand it.

The Wicked Son, what does he say?

"What is this service to you?"

"To you," [he says] and not to him.

When he takes himself out from the community, he makes [himself] a heretic.

And you must set his teeth on edge and say to him:

"Because of this the Lord acted for me when I came out of Egypt."

"For me", and not for him.

Had he been there, he would not have been redeemed.

---

community. In so doing, the Wicked Son denies an important part of Judaism. Judaism is a collective religion. There are many examples of religious duties that need to be done with a group, including many of the daily prayers, reading from the Torah, and saying *Kaddish*. On a deeper level though, as history understanding of Judaism; he does not know, not because he is bad, but because he was not given the opportunity to learn. The Son Who Does Not Know How to Ask is the one who knows so little that he cannot even participate. This sounds like a rather dysfunctional family, and therefore a dysfunctional Jewish community, but there is a message of hope here. All these sons are sitting at the table together. Therefore, there is the opportunity to engage all of them, at the level that is appropriate for each. In so doing, each child, and each member of the community, has the opportunity to learn from each other. The Jewish community can be strengthened by all its members.

חָכָם, מָה הוּא אוֹמֵר?
מָה הָעֵדֹת וְהַחֻקִּים וְהַמִּשְׁפָּטִים
אֲשֶׁר צִוָּה יְהֹוָה אֱלֹהֵינוּ אֶתְכֶם?
וְאַף אַתָּה אֱמָר לוֹ כְּהִלְכוֹת הַפֶּסַח:
אֵין מַפְטִירִין אַחַר הַפֶּסַח אֲפִיקוֹמָן.

What makes the Wise Son's question so wise?

The Wise Son distinguishes between "testimonies", "statutes" and "laws". Testimonies are the commandments that relate to God's presence in the world, such as the Sabbath and Festivals. Statutes are the commandments that have no obvious reason, but which demonstrate Jewish faith in God, such as not mixing milk and meat. Laws are the commandments that relate to social justice, and which are knowable by all people, such as giving charity. The Wise Son is obviously at a very high level of observance and answering him requires an equally high level of explanation.

רָשָׁע, מָה הוּא אוֹמֵר?
מָה הָעֲבֹדָה הַזֹּאת לָכֶם?
לָכֶם– וְלֹא לוֹ.
וּלְפִי שֶׁהוֹצִיא אֶת עַצְמוֹ מִן הַכְּלָל כָּפַר בְּעִקָּר.
וְאַף אַתָּה הַקְהֵה אֶת שִׁנָּיו וֶאֱמָר לוֹ:
בַּעֲבוּר זֶה עָשָׂה יְהֹוָה לִי בְּצֵאתִי מִמִּצְרָיִם.
לִי– וְלֹא לוֹ.
אִלּוּ הָיָה שָׁם לֹא הָיָה נִגְאָל.

Why is the Wicked Son's question seen as wicked?

The Wicked Son's question is wicked because it shows he is rebelling against Judaism. He should say, "What is this service to us?" Instead, he phrases his question as "to you", excluding himself from the free society. History has shown that in such a society the powerful will take advantage of the weak. The difference between serving Pharaoh and serving God is that Pharaoh represents injustice, and God represents justice. In a society governed by the laws of God, the weak (such as the widow, orphan and stranger) will be protected.

Why is the Wicked Son wicked for saying "you", but the Wise Son is not wicked for saying "you"?

The difference is that the Wise Son asks his question saying "which our God commanded you." Rashi notes that the Wise Son does not exclude himself with the word "you" because he says "our God". This shows that he recognizes his own relationship to God.

The Simple Son, what does he say?

"What is this?"

And you must tell him:

"With a strong hand the Lord brought us out of Egypt, from the house of slavery."

Why is the response, "with a strong hand" an appropriate response to the Simple Son's question?

The Simple Son needs a simple response. The quote "with a strong hand" alludes to the very powerful and visible way in which God redeemed the Jewish people. He did so with miracles. People with a strong faith have no need for miracles. However, the simple story of the miracles of the Exodus is an appropriate answer for the Simple Son.

And the Son Who Does Not Know How to Ask, what does he say?

You must open [the story] for him, as it is said:

"And you shall tell your child on that day, saying:

'Because of this the Lord acted for me when I came out of Egypt.'"

How might the Son Who Does Not Know How to Ask be worse than the Wicked Son?

One potential problem with the Son Who Does Not Know How to Ask is that he may be ignorant. Being ignorant makes him almost totally cut off from Judaism, because he cannot even engage in the normal questioning and answering that is so important in our religion. Although the Wicked Son may be challenging, at least he asks important questions. He may seem dismissive, but in asking, he is at least open to an answer. The Wicked Son can therefore be convinced, and therefore can be brought back to proper observance. The *Haggadah*, in placing him last in the Four Sons, seems to be saying that the Son Who Does Not Know How to Ask is the worst of all.

has shown, the Jewish people cannot stand alone. We owe a responsibility to each other, and we share a collective fate. Even Jews who are not religious can feel an incredibly strong connection to and responsibility for the whole Jewish people. What makes the Wicked Son so wicked is not that he does not practice Judaism, but that he has divorced himself from the Jewish people.

Why does the Wicked Son use the word "*avoda*" [service], which also means "slavery", when referring to "this service" (that is, the Passover offering)?

The Wicked Son uses the word "*avoda*", which is the same word for slavery, as if to say that the Jewish people simply exchanged service of Pharaoh for service of God. He seems to believe that to really be free is to have no master, and to be subject to no rules. However, a society that has no rules is not a

---

תָּם, מָה הוּא אוֹמֵר?

מַה זֹּאת?

וְאָמַרְתָּ אֵלָיו:

בְּחֹזֶק יָד הוֹצִיאָנוּ יְהֹוָה מִמִּצְרַיִם מִבֵּית עֲבָדִים.

Q&A

Why is "What is this" a simple question, and what does it teach us about the way we should teach children?

"What is this?" is a simple question because it is only asking about the most basic level of the story. It is not a deep question or challenging question. However, every question deserves a response. Parents should not simply focus on the wise children, or as they often do, the wicked children. All children deserve the attention of parents. We may start off with a simple answer for the Simple Son, but as time goes on, the Simple Son will learn and grow. As parents, we have a duty to teach all our children in ways that are appropriate for them.

וְשֶׁאֵינוֹ יוֹדֵעַ לִשְׁאֹל, מָה הוּא אוֹמֵר?

אַתְּ פְּתַח לוֹ, שֶׁנֶּאֱמַר:

וְהִגַּדְתָּ לְבִנְךָ בַּיּוֹם הַהוּא לֵאמֹר,

בַּעֲבוּר זֶה עָשָׂה יְהֹוָה לִי בְּצֵאתִי מִמִּצְרָיִם.

What lesson does the Son Who Does Not Know How to Ask teach us?

A child who does not know how to ask is silent. Such a child requires special attention. There may be many reasons why children are silent. We need to spend the time to understand what the reasons for their silence are and address them. In the situation of the *seder*, we must have the right response to engage silent children and bring them out of their silence, because only through a dialogue of questions and answers can children learn and ultimately feel connected to Passover.

One might [have thought this meant] from the beginning of the month.

And so it says, "on that day".

Had it only said "on that day",

one might have thought it applied during the day.

And so it also says, "Because of this" –

"Because of this" can only be said

when matzah and bitter herbs are resting [there] before you.

---

to tell your child can only be fulfilled when the symbolic foods are before you at the *seder*. For a parent with a young child – the quintessential child who does not know how to ask – this is a very important point. Young children are likely to fall asleep early, perhaps even missing the *seder* itself. A parent of a young child might think it appropriate to begin telling the story of the Exodus before the *seder* to be certain to fulfill the *mitzvah*. However, the *Haggadah* explicitly tells us that we only fulfill the *mitzvah* when we tell our children the story of the Exodus at the *seder* itself, when the *matzah* and *maror* are on the table before us.

What other meaning can we derive from this passage?

Among the most famous declarations of the Jewish people was, "we will do and we will hear" [נַעֲשֶׂה וְנִשְׁמָע], which the Israelites declared upon Moses' reading the Book of the Covenant to the people. On a simple level, as Rashi explained, this means that the Jewish people accepted the covenant even before hearing its terms, such was the high level of their faith. On a deeper level, this declaration speaks of the necessity to act. Many people hear things and do nothing in response. That is not the Jewish way. Our ancestors demonstrated that Judaism must be lived. This passage hints at this idea. The story of the Exodus is relayed at the time we reenact it – at the *seder* table – when the "*matzah* and bitter herbs are there before you". We ensure each generation feels a connection to Judaism when they share in these ritual acts, not simply when they hear about them.

In the beginning

our ancestors were idol worshippers.

But now the Omnipresent has drawn us close in to His service.

As it is said,

"Joshua said to all the people,

'This is what the Lord, God of Israel, has said:

Beyond the river your ancestors always dwelled –

Terah, the father of Abraham, and the father of Nahor –

and they served other gods.

But I took your father Abraham from beyond the river,

יָכוֹל מֵרֹאשׁ חֹדֶשׁ.
תַּלְמוּד לוֹמַר בַּיּוֹם הַהוּא.
אִי בַּיּוֹם הַהוּא,
יָכוֹל מִבְּעוֹד יוֹם.
תַּלְמוּד לוֹמַר בַּעֲבוּר זֶה–
בַּעֲבוּר זֶה לֹא אָמַרְתִּי
אֶלָּא בְּשָׁעָה שֶׁיֵּשׁ מַצָּה וּמָרוֹר מֻנָּחִים לְפָנֶיךָ.

Q&A

What is this section, "One might [have thought this meant]", referring to?
This section is referring to the obligation "You shall tell [וְהִגַּדְתָּ] your child on that day", which is the obligation to tell the story of the Exodus.

Why does this passage follow the Four Sons?
We have just learned that the correct way of dealing with a child Who Does Not Know How to Ask is to say, "and you shall tell your child on that day, 'Because of this the Lord acted for me when I came out of Egypt.'" The *Haggadah* immediately provides an exegesis, or critical explanation, of this Torah commandment. It is an example of the type of analysis of the texts included in the *seder* in which the participants are meant to engage.

Why does this passage follow the Son Who Does Not Know How to Ask?
On its face, this is a very challenging passage to comprehend, far above the ability of a child Who Does Not Know How to Ask could understand. However, the passage is not meant to educate such a child, but rather to educate the parent. Preparations for Passover begin many days before the start of the festival. One might think from this that you can tell your child the story of the Exodus once preparations for the holiday begin. However, the Torah states "on that day", which means on the holiday itself. Lest one think that "on that day" means any time on that day, "because of this" clarifies that the obligation

מִתְּחִלָּה
עוֹבְדֵי עֲבוֹדָה זָרָה הָיוּ אֲבוֹתֵינוּ.
וְעַכְשָׁו קֵרְבָנוּ הַמָּקוֹם לַעֲבוֹדָתוֹ.
שֶׁנֶּאֱמַר:
וַיֹּאמֶר יְהוֹשֻׁעַ אֶל כָּל הָעָם,
כֹּה אָמַר יְהֹוָה אֱלֹהֵי יִשְׂרָאֵל:
בְּעֵבֶר הַנָּהָר יָשְׁבוּ אֲבוֹתֵיכֶם מֵעוֹלָם,
תֶּרַח אֲבִי אַבְרָהָם וַאֲבִי נָחוֹר,
וַיַּעַבְדוּ אֱלֹהִים אֲחֵרִים.
וָאֶקַּח אֶת אֲבִיכֶם אֶת אַבְרָהָם מֵעֵבֶר הַנָּהָר,

and I led him all the way across the land of Canaan,
and I multiplied his offspring and gave him Isaac.
And to Isaac I gave Jacob and Esau,
and I gave Esau Mount Seir as an inheritance,
while Jacob and his children went down to Egypt.' "

What is the significance of Joshua's speech at this point in the *Haggadah*?

This is a passage from Joshua's farewell speech to the Jewish people. Joshua feared that the Jewish people might assimilate into the surrounding inhabitants of Canaan. In order to inspire the Jewish people with hope and faith, he told the story of how Abraham and his descendants were liberated from idolatry. This is particularly relevant to Jewish people today who are faced with the dangers of assimilation into their surrounding cultures. We all must struggle, just like Abraham, for spiritual freedom, and take heart that we can succeed like our forefathers.

Blessed is the One who has kept His promise to Israel,
blessed is He.
For the Holy One, blessed is he,
calculated the end [of the exile] and fulfilled what He had said
to Abraham, our father, in the Covenant between the Pieces.
As it is said:
"He said to Abram,
'Know that your descendants will be strangers in a land not their own,
and they will be enslaved and oppressed for four hundred years.
But [know] also that I shall judge the nation that enslaves them,
and afterwards they will go out with great wealth.' "

Why are there two different calculations for the length of the Jewish people's slavery?

God foretold that the Jewish people would be "strangers in a land not their own", "enslaved" and "oppressed" for a period of 400 hundred years. However, the slavery in Egypt was only 210 years (based on the lineages set out in the Torah). The sages explain that the 400 years began not with the enslavement, but at the time that the descendants of Abraham were "strangers in a land not their own". This means that the 400-year period began at the birth of Isaac, who was a "stranger" in Canaan. The 210 years of enslavement is also hinted at in Jacob's instructions to his children to go down to Egypt: "Go down [רְדוּ] there and buy [food]". The numerical value of ר-ד-ו is 210.

וָאוֹלֵךְ אֹתוֹ בְּכָל אֶרֶץ כְּנָעַן,
וָאַרְבֶּה אֶת זַרְעוֹ וָאֶתֵּן לוֹ אֶת יִצְחָק.
וָאֶתֵּן לְיִצְחָק אֶת יַעֲקֹב וְאֶת עֵשָׂו,
וָאֶתֵּן לְעֵשָׂו אֶת הַר שֵׂעִיר לָרֶשֶׁת אוֹתוֹ,
וְיַעֲקֹב וּבָנָיו יָרְדוּ מִצְרָיִם.

Q&A

What does the fact that our ancestors were "idol worshippers" have to do with the story of the Exodus?

As discussed above, there are two views on how to fulfill the Mishnaic obligation that the telling of the Exodus must "begin with the shame and end with the praise". The first is that of Shmuel, who believed that the main theme of the *seder* is of the Jewish people's physical redemption (and therefore the previous section starts with "we were slaves"). His contemporary, Rav, held the view that the obligation is fulfilled by emphasizing the theme of spiritual redemption. Therefore, the *Haggadah* focuses here on spiritual servitude and starts with "our ancestors were idol worshippers".

בָּרוּךְ שׁוֹמֵר הַבְטָחָתוֹ לְיִשְׂרָאֵל,
בָּרוּךְ הוּא.
שֶׁהַקָּדוֹשׁ בָּרוּךְ הוּא
חִשַּׁב אֶת הַקֵּץ לַעֲשׂוֹת כְּמָה שֶׁאָמַר
לְאַבְרָהָם אָבִינוּ בִּבְרִית בֵּין הַבְּתָרִים.
שֶׁנֶּאֱמַר:
וַיֹּאמֶר לְאַבְרָם,
יָדֹעַ תֵּדַע כִּי גֵר יִהְיֶה זַרְעֲךָ בְּאֶרֶץ לֹא לָהֶם,
וַעֲבָדוּם וְעִנּוּ אֹתָם אַרְבַּע מֵאוֹת שָׁנָה.
וְגַם אֶת הַגּוֹי אֲשֶׁר יַעֲבֹדוּ דָּן אָנֹכִי,
וְאַחֲרֵי כֵן יֵצְאוּ בִּרְכֻשׁ גָּדוֹל.

Q&A

What is the meaning and purpose of this section?

After the previous section, which tells of the spiritual ascent of the Jewish people from idol worship to belief in God, this section tells of the physical descent of the Jewish people into slavery in Egypt. The purpose though, by describing how Abraham's descendants will ultimately leave with great wealth and that the Egyptian slavers will be "judged", is meant to provide assurance of God's divine protection. It provides a comforting message that no matter what the ups and downs in Jewish life, God will protect the Jewish people.

Cover the matzot.
All participants raise their wine glasses.

For a transliteration of the Hebrew text, please turn to page 170.

And this is what has stood

by our ancestors and us:

For it has not been only one [nation] that has risen up to destroy us,

but in every generation [nations] rise up to destroy us,

but the Holy One, blessed is He, saves us from their hands.

Put down the wine cups and uncover the matzot.

Why does this section refer to every generation being subject to a nation that seeks to destroy us?

Egypt was only the first nation that sought to destroy the Jewish people. They were not the last. By the time of the compilation of the *Haggadah* there had already been multiple nations that had sought our destruction. And not just any nations, but some of the greatest nations of the ancient world: Assyria, Babylon, the Greek Seleucids, and the Romans. Some of these nations came perilously close. Assyria destroyed the Kingdom of Israel, scattering the ten tribes of the north who for the most part have remained lost to history. Babylon destroyed the First Temple, and exiled much of the population to the east. The Greek Seleucids attempted to destroy the Jewish people by forbidding key Jewish practices, such as circumcision. The Romans destroyed the Second Temple, raised countless cities and villages, and killed or exiled most of the population. Few, if any peoples would have survived even one such event. Yet the Jewish people defied destruction and carried on. The list of other nations that subsequently attempted to exterminate the Jewish people, and the massacres, pogroms and holocausts that have occurred since Roman times is long indeed. "But the Holy One, blessed is He, saves us from their hands." This section reminds us that no matter what tragedy may befall us, God maintains a special bond that ensures our communal redemption from even the darkest tragedies that may befall us.

Go out and learn

what Lavan the Aramean sought to do to Jacob, our father.

Pharaoh condemned only the boys [to death],

but Lavan sought to uproot everything.

As it is written:

"An Aramean [sought to] destroy my forefather,

and he went down to Egypt

and sojourned there with a small number of people,

and there he became a nation, great, mighty, and numerous.

And the Egyptians treated us cruelly and oppressed us,

Cover the מצות.
All participants raise their wine glasses.

For a transliteration of the following text, please turn to page 170.

וְהִיא שֶׁעָמְדָה

לַאֲבוֹתֵינוּ וְלָנוּ:
שֶׁלֹּא אֶחָד בִּלְבַד עָמַד עָלֵינוּ לְכַלּוֹתֵנוּ,
אֶלָּא שֶׁבְּכָל דּוֹר וָדוֹר עוֹמְדִים עָלֵינוּ לְכַלּוֹתֵנוּ,
וְהַקָּדוֹשׁ בָּרוּךְ הוּא מַצִּילֵנוּ מִיָּדָם.

Put down the wine cups and uncover the מצות.

Q&A

What does "And this" refer to?

We have just read above about God's promise to Avram that his descendants would be redeemed from slavery. Therefore, on a simple level, "And this" refers to God's promise to redeem us. However, there is a second deeper meaning that comes from the Arizal, who said that "And this" refers to our reserves of faith. When we have faith in God, then God will also have faith in us. When God has faith in us, He keeps His promise to save us from our enemies.

Why do we raise our wine glasses?

The four cups of wine correspond to the four promises made by God, "And I will bring you out, and I will redeem you, and I will save you, and I will take you." The second cup corresponds to the promise of "redemption". Wine is a common medium for expressing our joy, and nothing is more worthy of joyful acknowledgment than our own salvation from slavery. As the Psalmist wrote in Psalm 116, "I will lift up the cup of salvation". And so we too lift our cup here in recognition of God's salvation, which this paragraph highlights.

צֵא וּלְמַד

מַה בִּקֵּשׁ לָבָן הָאֲרַמִּי לַעֲשׂוֹת לְיַעֲקֹב אָבִינוּ.
שֶׁפַּרְעֹה לֹא גָזַר אֶלָּא עַל הַזְּכָרִים,
וְלָבָן בִּקֵּשׁ לַעֲקֹר אֶת הַכֹּל.
שֶׁנֶּאֱמַר:
אֲרַמִּי אֹבֵד אָבִי,
וַיֵּרֶד מִצְרַיְמָה
וַיָּגָר שָׁם בִּמְתֵי מְעָט,
וַיְהִי שָׁם לְגוֹי גָּדוֹל, עָצוּם וָרָב.
וַיָּרֵעוּ אֹתָנוּ הַמִּצְרִים וַיְעַנּוּנוּ,

and imposed hard labor upon us.
And we cried out to the Lord, God of our forefathers, and the Lord heard our voice
and saw our affliction, our toil, and our stress.
And the Lord brought us out from Egypt
with a strong hand and with an outstretched arm,
with great awe, and with signs and with wonders."

Why were these verses included in the *Haggadah*?

These words were well known to Jews in the times of the Temple. Coming from the book of Deuteronomy, they were recited at the time of the giving of the first fruits during the Shavuot holiday. Immediately before reciting these words, Jews would recite another verse, which states "And you shall come to the *kohen* who will be [serving] in those days, and say to him, 'I declare [הִגַּדְתִּי] this day to the Lord, your God, that I have come to the land which the Lord swore to our forefathers to give us.'" The sages who added this section to the *Haggadah* may have believed that it was not a coincidence that the word "declare" [הִגַּדְתִּי] has the same root [ה-ג-ד] as "Hagaddah" [הַגָּדָה] and therefore chose to include the words that were commanded to be said in the *Haggadah* itself.

What is the connection between these verses and the story of the Exodus?

When coming to offer first fruits at the time of the Festival of Shavuot, the Book of Deuteronomy commands the Jews to recite these verses, which describe the Jewish people's journey down to Egypt, its enslavement, and eventual redemption by God. The culmination of this redemption was entering the Land of Israel. This is essentially an acknowledgment of God's blessings, the faith of the Jewish people, and the care God takes for us, all of which have a clear connection to the overarching message of the story of the Exodus.

As it is written:
"An Aramean [sought to] destroy my forefather,
and he went down to Egypt
and sojourned there with a small number of people,
and there he became a nation, great, mighty and numerous."

So important are these rules to religious life, they have been made part of the morning service, and are recited in their entirety before *Pesukei D'zimrah*. This section of the *Haggadah* more than any other befuddles and confuses modern readers. It is the most extended example of the type of hermeneutics in which the sages routinely would engage, and in which we are all called upon to engage at the *seder*.

וַיִּתְּנוּ עָלֵינוּ עֲבֹדָה קָשָׁה.
וַנִּצְעַק אֶל יְהֹוָה אֱלֹהֵי אֲבֹתֵינוּ, וַיִּשְׁמַע יְהֹוָה אֶת קֹלֵנוּ
וַיַּרְא אֶת עָנְיֵנוּ וְאֶת עֲמָלֵנוּ וְאֶת לַחֲצֵנוּ.
וַיּוֹצִאֵנוּ יְהֹוָה מִמִּצְרַיִם
בְּיָד חֲזָקָה וּבִזְרֹעַ נְטוּיָה
וּבְמֹרָא גָּדֹל, וּבְאֹתוֹת וּבְמֹפְתִים.

Q&A

Why should we "go out and learn"?

The previous section told us that in every generation a nation rises up to destroy us, but that God ultimately saves us. In case one has any doubt, the *Haggadah* seems to be saying, "go out and learn" and you will see that in fact this is true. The *Haggadah* then goes on to relate two well-known examples of attempts to destroy our ancestors, and in both cases God saved us.

How was Lavan worse than Pharaoh?

While it is true that Pharaoh oppressed the Jewish people and enslaved them, these actions only served to strengthen them. The Torah states "the more they were oppressed, the more they multiplied and spread." In contrast, Lavan's actions would have destroyed the Jewish people. He did not oppress Jacob. In fact, Jacob grew wealthy and comfortable in life while with Lavan. Had Jacob remained with Lavan, he may eventually have forgotten what was truly important. These two themes of oppression and comfort in Jewish history recur over and over. When times are difficult, the Jewish people pull together, but when times are easy, Jews assimilate and disappear. Moses provided the Jewish people a warning against this danger when he said "Be careful that you do not forget the Lord your God. Otherwise, when you eat and are satisfied, when you build fine houses and settle down, and when your herds and flocks grow large and your silver and gold increase and all you have is multiplied, then you will become proud and you will forget the Lord your God, who brought you out of Egypt, out of the land of slavery."

שֶׁנֶּאֱמַר:
אֲרַמִּי אֹבֵד אָבִי,
וַיֵּרֶד מִצְרַיְמָה
וַיָּגָר שָׁם בִּמְתֵי מְעָט,
וַיְהִי שָׁם לְגוֹי גָּדוֹל, עָצוּם וָרָב.

Q&A

What is "hermeneutics"?

Hermeneutics is a methodology used to interpret a religious text. The primary task of hermeneutics is to understand a text's relevance to the present. The classical enumeration of Jewish hermeneutics is the set of 13 rules for interpreting the Torah compiled by Rabbi Yishmael, who lived in the 2nd century CE. The rules demonstrate how the Oral Law, laid out in the Talmud, can be derived from the Torah itself.

"And he went down to Egypt"

Compelled on account of the decree.

God tells him to have no fear about going to Egypt, because He would make him into a "great nation". God also provided divine assurance that just as Jacob would go down to Egypt, God would also bring him up from there. The story does not mention what Jacob's fear was, but from God's response, it is clear that Jacob feared that he was descending into the exile that had been prophesied to both Abraham and Isaac. The "decree", which compelled him, was this prophesy.

"And sojourned there"

From this, learn that Jacob, our father, did not go down

to settle in Egypt,

but rather to sojourn (live temporarily) there.

As it is said:

"They said to Pharaoh,

'We have come to sojourn in this land,

for there is no pasture for your servants' flocks,

for the famine is heavy in the land of Canaan.

And now, if you please, let your servants dwell in the land of Goshen.' "

What can we learn from the fact the stay ended up not being temporary?

When the exiles were marched from the land of Israel to Babylon, the Psalmist writes the haunting lines "How shall we sing the song of the Lord on foreign soil? If I forget you, O Jerusalem, ... may my tongue cling to my palate, if I do not remember you, if I do not bring up Jerusalem at the beginning of my joy!" Yet within just two generations, the exiles had not only made a home in Babylon, but thrived there. So comfortable were the exiles in their new land that only a small remnant went to Israel with the Prophet Ezra when the Persian King, Cyrus the Great, permitted their return. Life in Babylon, just as life in Egypt, was good. This has been a recurring pattern of Jewish life throughout history, with Moorish Spain, medieval England, Ottoman Turkey, and Poland, being but a few examples of places that once welcomed, and then rejected Jewish communities. Intentions are important, but they are only words unless they are acted upon.

"With a small number of people"

As it is said:

"Your ancestors were seventy souls when they went down to Egypt,

וַיֵּרֶד מִצְרַיְמָה–

אָנוּס עַל פִּי הַדִּבּוּר.

Q&A

What was the decree that compelled Jacob to go down to Egypt?

The simple reason Jacob went down to Egypt was that a famine had struck Canaan. Egypt offered not only the opportunity to get much needed food, but also the opportunity to reunite with his long–lost, and much beloved son, Joseph, who had risen to become second in command of Egypt. However, a deeper look into the story reveals that before leaving Canaan, Jacob had a vision of God. In this vision,

---

וַיָּגָר שָׁם–

מְלַמֵּד שֶׁלֹּא יָרַד יַעֲקֹב אָבִינוּ
לְהִשְׁתַּקֵּעַ בְּמִצְרַיִם,
אֶלָּא לָגוּר שָׁם.
שֶׁנֶּאֱמַר:
וַיֹּאמְרוּ אֶל פַּרְעֹה,
לָגוּר בָּאָרֶץ בָּאנוּ,
כִּי אֵין מִרְעֶה לַצֹּאן אֲשֶׁר לַעֲבָדֶיךָ,
כִּי כָבֵד הָרָעָב בְּאֶרֶץ כְּנָעַן.
וְעַתָּה יֵשְׁבוּ נָא עֲבָדֶיךָ בְּאֶרֶץ גֹּשֶׁן.

Q&A

How do we know that Jacob only intended to stay temporarily in Egypt?

Chapter 47 of Genesis tells us that Jacob lived for 17 years in Egypt. This would seem to suggest something more than a temporary stay. However, our sages agree that the intention was only to remain in Egypt temporarily. The use of the word "*vayagar*" is interpreted as "sojourn", meaning a transient stay, rather than a permanent settlement. As Jacob's children explained to Pharaoh when they met, their reason for coming to Egypt was predicated on exigent and temporary circumstances related to the famine in Canaan. They merely sought to "dwell" in Goshen until conditions in Canaan improved.

בִּמְתֵי מְעָט–

כְּמָה שֶׁנֶּאֱמַר:

בְּשִׁבְעִים נֶפֶשׁ יָרְדוּ אֲבוֹתֶיךָ מִצְרָיְמָה,

and now the Lord, your God, has made you

as numerous as the stars of the sky."

---

set up the boundaries of [i.e. established the] peoples according to the number of the children of Israel." There are many other instances of the number 70 in the *Tanach*. Seventy is the number of elders that assisted Moses in the desert, as well as the number of judges that constituted the Sanhedrin. The Sages stated that the Torah has 70 "faces" or ways to understand it. A person who has reached 70 years has lived a normal span of life, as the psalmist stated in Psalm 90. The number 70 can therefore be thought as symbolizing completeness: with respect to the nations of the world, the Jewish nation, the judicial authority of the Jewish nation, the binding authority regarding interpretation of the Torah, and of life itself.

"And there he became a nation"

From this, learn that Israel was distinct there.

---

where Jews who settle in new lands take on local names, speak the local language (and for the most part do not know Hebrew), and assimilate into the practices of the dominant cultural milieu. Despite being in the most powerful society of the ancient world, and even becoming enslaved by that society, the Israelites in Egypt fiercely maintained their cultural identity. This should be an example to all Jewish people today that no matter what forces, be they benign or malignant, which are arrayed against us, keeping our cultural identity intact is the key to Jewish unity and longevity. Lest this message of distinctness be taken too far, to a point of isolation and disengagement from wider society, Rabbi Menachem Mendel Schneerson encouraged Jews to maintain their identity not just by sanctifying every aspect of our lives, but also by positively engaging with and influencing the wider world, thereby sanctifying it as well.

"Great, mighty"

As it is said:

"And the children of Israel were fertile,

and they swarmed, and grew more and more numerous, and strong,

and the land was filled with them."

---

possible. The traditional approach to rationalizing this rapid population growth was the belief that women gave birth to large numbers of children. The medieval commentator, Rashi, stated that women regularly gave birth to sextuplets. At this rate, starting from 70 couples, each couple having two pregnancies, each of six children, and repeating for several generations, there would be millions of descendants. That

וְעַתָּה שָׂמְךָ יְהֹוָה אֱלֹהֶיךָ
כְּכוֹכְבֵי הַשָּׁמַיִם לָרֹב.

Q&A

Who was the 70th person whose name is unmentioned in the Torah?

In Chapter 46 of the book of Exodus, we are told that "all the souls of the house of Jacob who came down to Egypt were seventy." However, a careful reading of the names listed amounts to only 69. Various commentators have suggested that the 70th person was Yocheved, the mother of Moses, who was born on the way down to Egypt. However, as with many numbers in the *Tanach*, the number 70 may not be literal. It would not be lost on a close reader of the *Tanach* that the 70 who came down to Egypt matches numerically the 70 nations descended from Noah. As it states in Deuteronomy, chapter 32, "He [God]

וַיְהִי שָׁם לְגוֹי –

מְלַמֵּד שֶׁהָיוּ יִשְׂרָאֵל מְצֻיָּנִים שָׁם.

Q&A

How did Israel remain distinct in Egypt?

When Jacob and his household arrived in Egypt they settled in the land of Goshen, which is believed to be in the northeast of Egypt, and distant from the then capital, Thebes, south of modern day Cairo. When Joseph introduced his brothers to Pharaoh, they made a point of identifying themselves as shepherds, a profession associated with nomads and which the more urban and agricultural Egyptians looked down upon. From this it is clear that the Israelites chose to dwell apart from the Egyptians and maintain their distinct way of life. The sages also identified several ways in which the Israelites remained distinct as the years progressed. It is said that they continued to speak their language, kept their culture alive, and did not change their names or their dress. Such practices stand in marked contrast to the modern way of life

---

גָּדוֹל, עָצוּם –

כְּמָה שֶׁנֶּאֱמַר:
וּבְנֵי יִשְׂרָאֵל פָּרוּ,
וַיִּשְׁרְצוּ וַיִּרְבּוּ וַיַּעַצְמוּ בִּמְאֹד מְאֹד,
וַתִּמָּלֵא הָאָרֶץ אֹתָם.

Q&A

How could the Israelites have become so numerous?

Seventy people from the house of Jacob are recorded as having gone down to Egypt. Two hundred ten years later, the census of the Israelites in the book of Numbers following the Exodus recorded a population of 603,550 men 20 years and older. Including women and children, this would suggest a total population of at least 3 million. Even pre-modern biblical commentators wondered how this was

One way of understanding the census of 603,550 adult men is to translate the word "*eleph*", which is traditionally translated as "thousand", as a "troop" or "clan", and "*ve*", which is normally translated as "and", as "or". For example, in the census, when the tribe of Judah is counted as "seventy-four *eleph*, *ve* six hundred", we should read this not as seventy-four thousand and six hundred [adult men], but as "seventy-four clans, or 600 [adult men]". Thus, the census would have counted a total of 598 clans, made up of 5,550 adult men. This approach is consistent with other uses of the word "*eleph*" in the *Tanach* where it more clearly means a "troop" or "clan", such as in Joshua 22:14 ("They were each one the head of the house of their fathers, among the clans of Israel") and Judges 6:15 ("Behold, my troop [clan] is the poorest in Menashe, and I am the youngest in my father's household."), as well as other uses of the word "*ve*" where it means "or". Some consider this interpretation to be a stretch of the Hebrew, and prefer to treat what clearly are fantastically high numbers merely as symbolic of a large number of people. Viewing the Israelites as much smaller in number is also consistent with Moses' statement in the book of Deuteronomy that "the Lord did not set His affection on you and choose you because you were more numerous than other peoples, for you are the fewest of all peoples."

"And numerous"

As it is said:

"And I passed over you

and I saw you wallowing in your blood,

and I said to you, 'By your blood, live!'

And I said to you, 'By your blood, live!'

I caused you to grow wild like plants of the field,

and you grew and matured and became adorned,

your breasts full and your hair grown,

yet you were naked and barren."

---

which they would have merited redemption, so God gave them two *mitzvot*, the covenant of circumcision and the Passover offering, by which they earned their redemption through blood.

How is "numerous" proven by this passage?

Imagery of the fecundity of plants is ripe with symbolic meaning. In this passage from Ezekiel, the Jewish people are likened to plants of the field, which grow in the wild without the special care and attention required by domesticated plants. So too, Abarbanel noted that Jewish children in Egypt, despite the harsh conditions of slavery, and the lack of parental upbringing normally needed to attain high character, nevertheless thrived and developed. In this interpretation, "numerous" speaks to the manner of their development rather than sheer numbers, to which the previous term "great" referred.

seems like miraculous population growth. Rather than relying on a miracle, however, the proof text for the Israelites becoming "great" and "mighty" (i.e. numerous), likens their fertility to the phenomenon of swarming insects. Although an unflattering allusion, it nevertheless explains the astounding fertility of the children of Israel in a naturalistic manner.

Were the Israelites in fact so numerous?

For modern people, accustomed to cities with 10 million people or more, a Jewish population of 600,000, or even 3 million, seems entirely plausible. However, no biblical scholar accepts these numbers as factual. Based on a variety of archeological evidence, as well as the carrying capacity of Egypt's agricultural output, the entire population of ancient Egypt at the time of Ramses II is estimated to have been less than 3 million people in total. Given that the Judge, Deborah, only several generations after the Exodus, alludes in her song to only 40,000 men capable of bearing arms, the 603,550 counted in the census after the Exodus is difficult to accept outside of simple faith. Professor Richard Elliot Friedman also points out that even if the departing Israelites were walking eight abreast, by the time the front of the line got to Mount Sinai, half of the people would still have been in Egypt! How to resolve this?

וָרָב –

כְּמָה שֶׁנֶּאֱמַר:
וָאֶעֱבֹר עָלַיִךְ
וָאֶרְאֵךְ מִתְבּוֹסֶסֶת בְּדָמָיִךְ,
וָאֹמַר לָךְ בְּדָמַיִךְ חֲיִי,
וָאֹמַר לָךְ בְּדָמַיִךְ חֲיִי.
רְבָבָה כְּצֶמַח הַשָּׂדֶה נְתַתִּיךְ,
וַתִּרְבִּי וַתִּגְדְּלִי וַתָּבֹאִי בַּעֲדִי עֲדָיִים,
שָׁדַיִם נָכֹנוּ וּשְׂעָרֵךְ צִמֵּחַ,
וְאַתְּ עֵרֹם וְעֶרְיָה.

Q&A

What does this passage, "And I passed over you", mean and what is its relevance to the Exodus?

This passage is taken from the book of Ezekiel, a prophet and *kohen* who prophesied during the time of the destruction of the First Temple. In this passage, the Prophet metaphorically compared the city of Jerusalem, which had been laid waste, to a newborn child. Rather than seeing blood as a sign of death, Ezekiel likened it to a sign of life and the merit of the Jewish people. Jerusalem may have appeared to have died due to the devastation of the Babylonians – its streets literally filled with blood – but the double reference to "by your blood, live" reflects, according to Rashi, the merit for which redemption is due: the blood of circumcision and the blood of the Passover offering. The sages included this passage as a metaphor for the Exodus. The Israelites may have been "naked and barren", that is, without *mitzvot* by

"And the Egyptions treated us cruelly and oppressed us,
and imposed hard labor on us."

"And the Egyptians treated us cruelly"

As it is said:
"Let us act wisely towards them,
lest they multiply,
and when we are called to war,
they will join with our enemies,
and fight against us
and go up [to leave] from the land."

---

to violence – massacres, pogroms, and the Holocaust. This is a sequence of events that has been all too well known to Jewish communities throughout time.

Why would the Egyptians believe the Israelites would fight against them?

The descent of the Israelites into slavery was initiated by the belief that the Israelites posed a danger "from within". Historically, this has been a common charge leveled against Jewish communities. Jews were considered stateless outsiders, a potential fifth column that could align with foreign elements and undermine the state. The Egyptians, however, had reason to be concerned based on their own history. Egypt's 15th dynasty, which lasted from approximately 1650 to 1550 BCE, was founded by Western Asian peoples who had migrated to Northern Egypt. These people were known as the Hyskos (which is a Greek form of the Egyptian title, "Heka Khasut", meaning "rulers of foreign lands"). They, like the Israelites, also may have migrated due to the periodic famines that plague the Fertile Crescent because of poor rainfall. The Israelites, as a large group of foreigners, may have brought up uncomfortable memories of the Hyskos and the potential dangers to Egyptian rule.

"And oppressed us"

As it is said:

"They placed taskmasters over them

to oppress them with burdens.

And they built storage cities for Pharaoh, Pitom and Ramses."

וַיָּרֵעוּ אֹתָנוּ הַמִּצְרִים וַיְעַנּוּנוּ,
וַיִּתְּנוּ עָלֵינוּ עֲבֹדָה קָשָׁה.

וַיָּרֵעוּ אֹתָנוּ הַמִּצְרִים–

כְּמָה שֶׁנֶּאֱמַר:
הָבָה נִתְחַכְּמָה לוֹ,
פֶּן יִרְבֶּה,
וְהָיָה כִּי תִקְרֶאנָה מִלְחָמָה,
וְנוֹסַף גַּם הוּא עַל שֹׂנְאֵינוּ,
וְנִלְחַם בָּנוּ
וְעָלָה מִן הָאָרֶץ.

Why is the quoted verse proof that the Egyptians treated the Israelites cruelly?

This proof of the Egyptian cruelty towards the Israelites comes from a verse in Exodus, chapter 1, yet it seems only to provide a reason for the Egyptians' cruelty, rather than being an example of cruelty itself. One medieval commentator suggested then that the term should be read as meaning they "perceived" us cruelly. The quote then shows their perceived wisdom in deciding to treat the Israelites cruelly.

How did the Egyptians act "wisely" towards the Israelites?

The *midrash* relates that the Egyptians did not immediately enslave the Israelites. Rather, much like with the proverbial frog, the Egyptians slowly increased the temperature until it was too late for the Israelites to escape the boiling water. Slowly taking away rights and imposing obligations has been a common method of persecution of the Jewish people throughout history. Jews settle in a new land, often at the behest of the local ruler. Initially, life is good and the Jews prosper. Inevitably, the time comes when the Jews' success causes jealousy, and their separateness causes distrust. Small acts of discrimination – distinct clothing, like a pointed hat or yellow patch of cloth – lead to bigger acts – being forced to live behind walls, or prevented from entering certain professions or owning certain property – and ultimately

וַיְעַנּוּנוּ–

כְּמָה שֶׁנֶּאֱמַר:
וַיָּשִׂימוּ עָלָיו שָׂרֵי מִסִּים
לְמַעַן עַנֹּתוֹ בְּסִבְלֹתָם.
וַיִּבֶן עָרֵי מִסְכְּנוֹת לְפַרְעֹה אֶת פִּתֹם וְאֶת רַעַמְסֵס.

2924, or 837 BCE. This would put the Exodus in the year 1317 BCE, or almost 40 years before Ramses II's reign began. This mistiming is more acute given that biblical scholars generally date the beginning of King Solomon's reign to the middle of the 10th century, which would place the Exodus even more remotely in the past – well before the birth of Ramses II. However, it is possible that the 480 years is more symbolic than accurate. The Torah often refers to idealized generations of 40-year periods. The archetypal period is the 40 years the Israelites wandered in the desert, which was quite literally "a generation". This reading is supported by the not coincidental fact that both King Solomon and King David reigned for exactly 40 years. Modern people systematically date and record events, making it easy to pinpoint when they occurred. Ancient peoples were less exacting. Four hundred and eighty years may simply have meant 12 generations. This understanding easily allows for the Exodus to have occurred during the reign of Ramses II.

"And imposed hard labor on us"

As it is said:

"And the Egyptians enslaved the children of Israel with backbreaking work."

"And we cried out to the Lord, God of our forefathers,
and the Lord heard our voice,
and saw our affliction, our toil, and our stress."

"And we cried out to the Lord, God of our forefathers"

As it is said:

"It came to be, as a long time passed,
that the king of Egypt died
and the children of Israel groaned from [under the burden of] the work,
and they cried out,
and their plea rose to God from amid the work."

"And the Lord heard our voice"

As it is said:

"And God heard their groans,
and God remembered His covenant
with Abraham, Isaac and Jacob."

Q&A

How can these storage cities be used to date the Exodus?

The cities of Pitom and Ramses are well known to history and are referred to in both ancient Greek and Roman sources. Pitom means "House of Atum", Atum being an Egyptian deity associated with the sun disk. Because its location has not been definitively discovered, it is not possible to use it as a reference point to establish the date of the enslavement. Ramses corresponds to the city, "Pi-Ramses", which has been discovered, explored, and dated. Egyptologists believe it was built for Pharaoh Ramses II and served as his capital. This would place the historical Exodus during his reign, which lasted from 1279 – 1214 BCE. This suggests strongly that the Exodus occurred around the year 1250 BCE.

How can we reconcile the date of the Exodus during Ramses II's reign, with the timing set out in the Tanach?

The timing of the Exodus is set out in the first book of Kings, chapter 6. It states that King Solomon began his rule 480 years after the Exodus. Jewish tradition has Solomon becoming king in the year

---

וַיִּתְּנוּ עָלֵינוּ עֲבֹדָה קָשָׁה–

כְּמָה שֶׁנֶּאֱמַר:
וַיַּעֲבִדוּ מִצְרַיִם אֶת בְּנֵי יִשְׂרָאֵל בְּפָרֶךְ.

וַנִּצְעַק אֶל יְהֹוָה אֱלֹהֵי אֲבֹתֵינוּ,
וַיִּשְׁמַע יְהֹוָה אֶת קֹלֵנוּ,
וַיַּרְא אֶת עָנְיֵנוּ וְאֶת עֲמָלֵנוּ וְאֶת לַחֲצֵנוּ.

וַנִּצְעַק אֶל יְהֹוָה אֱלֹהֵי אֲבֹתֵינוּ–

כְּמָה שֶׁנֶּאֱמַר:
וַיְהִי בַיָּמִים הָרַבִּים הָהֵם,
וַיָּמָת מֶלֶךְ מִצְרַיִם,
וַיֵּאָנְחוּ בְנֵי יִשְׂרָאֵל מִן הָעֲבֹדָה,
וַיִּזְעָקוּ,
וַתַּעַל שַׁוְעָתָם אֶל הָאֱלֹהִים מִן הָעֲבֹדָה.

וַיִּשְׁמַע יְהֹוָה אֶת קֹלֵנוּ–

כְּמָה שֶׁנֶּאֱמַר:
וַיִּשְׁמַע אֱלֹהִים אֶת נַאֲקָתָם,
וַיִּזְכֹּר אֱלֹהִים אֶת בְּרִיתוֹ
אֶת אַבְרָהָם, אֶת יִצְחָק וְאֶת יַעֲקֹב.

Why would God "remember" as a result of hearing the Israelites' voice?

Rabbi Yehuda HaNasi, the redactor of the Mishnah, said that the Israelites lacked sufficient deeds, or *mitzvot*, to merit redemption by themselves. While they had maintained a distinct identity, they nevertheless were immersed in the culture of Egypt. The Israelites were particularly steeped in *avodah zarah*, idol worship, which was to have fateful repercussions in the incident of the golden calf. However, God heard the groans of the Israelites and remembered His covenant with our forefathers. It was on account of their meritorious deeds that God acted on behalf of the Israelites in slavery.

"And saw our affliction"

This [refers to] the separation from the 'way of the world'.

As it is said:

"And God saw the children of Israel, and God knew."

"*aneinu*" is also used in connection with Yom Kippur. On Yom Kippur we are commanded to "afflict" ourselves, meaning to refrain from sexual relations. Given that the Egyptians were repulsed by the rate of Jewish population growth, the sages understood that the Egyptians attempted to control this population growth by preventing Israelite families from procreating. The separation from the "way of the world" is a coy reference to the intimacy between man and wife.

"Our toil"

This [refers to] the sons.

As it is said:

"Throw every boy who is born into the river,

[but] let all the girls live."

to the Malbim, a 19th century commentator, Pharaoh wanted to keep the girls alive to satisfy his lustful urges. This view is consistent with traditional Jewish conceptions of Egypt as a morally corrupt society. Another view is that Pharaoh only wished to prevent the threat of an insurrection, which killing the boys would accomplish. However, killing the girls would have had the perverse effect of limiting his access to further slave labor. Perhaps an alternative reason is that Pharaoh believed that Jewishness passed through the men. Killing the boys would destroy the Jews, whereas killing the girls would have no effect. Whatever the reason, our sages agreed that it was not out of compassion that Pharaoh allowed the girls to live.

Q&A

What does it mean that the Lord "heard" the Israelites' voice?

The word "shema", which is translated as "hear", has a deeper meaning than simply to listen to something. When that word is used, for example, in "Hear, Israel, the Lord is our God, the Lord is one," it carries with it the connotation of hearing and acting accordingly. As Rabbi Lord Jonathan Sacks explained, Judaism requires more than blind obedience to rules. Rather, Judaism requires what Rabbi Sacks called "active listening". God did not simply hear the groans of the Israelites, He heard and was moved to fulfill His promise to redeem them from bondage.

וַיַּרְא אֶת עָנְיֵנוּ–

זוֹ פְּרִישׁוּת דֶּרֶךְ אֶרֶץ.

כְּמָה שֶׁנֶּאֱמַר:

וַיַּרְא אֱלֹהִים אֶת בְּנֵי יִשְׂרָאֵל וַיֵּדַע אֱלֹהִים.

Q&A

What does the "separation from the 'way of the world'" refer to?

We read above that the Egyptians *ya'aneinu*, "oppressed" us, which was interpreted to mean that we were "oppressed" with burdens. Yet, here again is the word in a different form, *aneinu*. As the same word is used again, the sages believed it must refer to a different type of oppression. In another example of the hermeneutics that is a hallmark of this section of the *Haggadah*, our sages noted that the word

---

וְאֶת עֲמָלֵנוּ–

אֵלּוּ הַבָּנִים.

כְּמָה שֶׁנֶּאֱמַר:

כָּל הַבֵּן הַיִּלּוֹד הַיְאֹרָה תַּשְׁלִיכֻהוּ,

וְכָל הַבַּת תְּחַיּוּן.

Q&A

Why does "toil" refer to the "sons"?

Toil is likened to sons because raising them requires toil. This fact is evident to anyone who has a son. Every aspect of raising sons requires effort, whether in difficult matters, such as mentoring and educating, or in seemingly mundane matters, such as listening to them. While raising girls also requires toil today, the sages lived in less progressively liberal times.

Why were only the boys killed?

There are several reasons offered for why Pharaoh decided to kill the boys and spare the girls. According

"Our stress"

This [refers to] the pressure.
As it is said:
"And I have seen the stress
that Egypt has forced on you."

"toil" refers to the sons, whose upbringing involves toil, "stress" refers to how the Egyptians made the Israelites work. According to Abarbanel, a 15th century Portuguese philosopher and commentator, the Egyptians constantly forced the Israelites to work more and more, without sufficient rest.

"And the Lord brought us out from Egypt
with a strong hand and with an outstretched arm,
with great awe, and with signs and with wonders."

"And the Lord brought us out from Egypt"

Not by the hand of an angel,
and not by the hand of a Seraph,
and not by the hand of a messenger.
Rather it was the Holy One, blessed is He, in His glory, Himself.
As it is said:
"I shall pass through the land of Egypt on that night.
I shall kill every firstborn son in the land of Egypt,
from [every] man to [every] beast,
and I shall pass judgment on all the gods of Egypt.
I am the Lord."
"And I shall pass through the land of Egypt" – I, and not an angel.
"And I shall kill every firstborn son" – I, and not a Seraph.
"And I shall pass judgment on all the gods of Egypt" – I, and not a messenger.
"I am the Lord" – I am Him, and there is no other.

אֶת לַחֲצֵנוּ–

זֶה הַדְּחַק.

כְּמָה שֶׁנֶּאֱמַר:

וְגַם רָאִיתִי אֶת הַלַּחַץ

אֲשֶׁר מִצְרַיִם לֹחֲצִים אֹתָם.

Q&A

What kind of “stress” did the Egyptians force upon the Israelites?

What seem like synonyms to describe slavery itself – affliction, toil, and stress – in fact describe distinct elements of slavery. While “affliction” refers to the prevention of intimacy between man and wife, and

---

וַיּוֹצִאֵנוּ יְהֹוָה מִמִּצְרַיִם

בְּיָד חֲזָקָה וּבִזְרֹעַ נְטוּיָה,

וּבְמֹרָא גָּדֹל, וּבְאֹתוֹת וּבְמֹפְתִים.

וַיּוֹצִאֵנוּ יְהֹוָה מִמִּצְרַיִם–

לֹא עַל יְדֵי מַלְאָךְ,

וְלֹא עַל יְדֵי שָׂרָף,

וְלֹא עַל יְדֵי שָׁלִיחַ,

אֶלָּא הַקָּדוֹשׁ בָּרוּךְ הוּא בִּכְבוֹדוֹ וּבְעַצְמוֹ.

שֶׁנֶּאֱמַר:

וְעָבַרְתִּי בְאֶרֶץ מִצְרַיִם בַּלַּיְלָה הַזֶּה.

וְהִכֵּיתִי כָל בְּכוֹר בְּאֶרֶץ מִצְרַיִם,

מֵאָדָם וְעַד בְּהֵמָה,

וּבְכָל אֱלֹהֵי מִצְרַיִם אֶעֱשֶׂה שְׁפָטִים.

אֲנִי יְהֹוָה.

וְעָבַרְתִּי בְאֶרֶץ מִצְרַיִם בַּלַּיְלָה הַזֶּה– אֲנִי וְלֹא מַלְאָךְ.

וְהִכֵּיתִי כָל בְּכוֹר בְּאֶרֶץ מִצְרַיִם– אֲנִי וְלֹא שָׂרָף.

וּבְכָל אֱלֹהֵי מִצְרַיִם אֶעֱשֶׂה שְׁפָטִים– אֲנִי ולֹא הַשָּׁלִיחַ.

אֲנִי יְהֹוָה– אֲנִי הוּא וְלֹא אַחֵר.

through Moses, his agent. Another reason for leaving Moses out is his part in the story is fixed in time. However, we are not conducting a *seder* simply to remember what happened in the past, but to make the Exodus relevant to the present. We are commanded to tell the story so that each of us can see ourselves as having gone personally out from Egypt. In whatever slavery we may find ourselves today, we do not need Moses to escape it. Only God can redeem us from our bondage. Other religions have as their focus a central founding figure, but the Jewish people look only to God.

Who are the "gods of Egypt" on whom God passed judgment?

Pagans of the ancient world believed that there were many gods. These gods were impersonal and personified natural forces or objects. Whether called Ra by the Egyptians, Shamash by the Babylonians, Helios and Sol by the Romans and Greeks, or whatever other name, the sun, as with many other objects, such as the moon and stars, were considered gods. So too elemental, universal forces, including "fertility", "war", "death" and others, were personified in the form of deities. Despite their impersonal nature, pagan gods were seen as worthy of worship, whether the god personified a mysterious and implacable force (like death) or a predictable and reliable object (like the sun). The process of bringing the Israelites out of Egypt – the plagues and miracles – was an exercise in overturning this worldview. Rather than many gods personifying different forces and objects, God demonstrated that all forces and all objects are in His control alone. Such was the judgment that God passed on the so-called "gods" of Egypt.

"With a strong hand"

This [refers to the] pestilence.

As it is said:

"Behold, the Hand of the Lord

upon the cattle in the field,

upon the horses, upon the donkeys, upon the camels,

upon the cattle and upon the flock,

an exceedingly heavy pestilence."

Egypt through the fifth plague of pestilence, but through the culminating tenth plague, the killing of the firstborn. This problem can be resolved, and the power of the fifth plague understood, from another statement in the Torah. God could have brought the Israelites out of Egypt through the fifth plague, but He refrained from annihilating the Egyptians with pestilence "to show you My strength and in order to declare My name over all the earth." Such was the power of the pestilence. Because all the plagues together were part of a lesson to teach the Egyptians that there is but one true God, He "hardened Pharaoh's heart", otherwise the pestilence alone would have caused Pharaoh to free the Israelites. Doing so would have been premature within the divine plan.

Q&A

What is an angel and what does it mean that an angel did not bring the Israelites out from Egypt?

In Hebrew, an angel is a "*mal'ach*", meaning a messenger. Angels appear throughout the Torah to deliver messages on behalf of God. Among the most famous angelic encounters are the three angels that visit Sarah to bring news that she will give birth; the angel that visits Hagar in the desert to assure her that her son, Yishmael, will live and become a father of a great nation; and the angel with whom Jacob wrestles and who renames him, Israel. While there are *midrashic* stories of angels arguing with God, the more commonly accepted idea is that angels do not act independently of God, but rather are merely an expression of His will. When the sages said that "the Lord brought us out of Egypt" and "not an angel", they were expressing the special attention that God bestowed on the Israelites. His care was so intimate that He did not send a messenger, but acted personally on our behalf.

Why is Moses not a central figure in the *Haggadah*?

The *Haggadah* mentions Moses' name only once, in the section in which the sages argue over the degree to which the miracle at the sea exceeded the ten plagues. However, given how integral Moses is to the story of the Exodus, this passing reference seems only to highlight his absence. The reason for Moses' absence from the story is simple. In much the same way as angels are merely messengers of God, Moses too was merely a messenger. Moses did not perform miracles, rather God performed miracles

---

בְּיָד חֲזָקָה–

זוֹ הַדֶּבֶר.

כְּמָה שֶׁנֶּאֱמַר:

הִנֵּה יַד יְהֹוָה

הוֹיָה בְּמִקְנְךָ אֲשֶׁר בַּשָּׂדֶה,

בַּסּוּסִים, בַּחֲמֹרִים, בַּגְּמַלִּים,

בַּבָּקָר וּבַצֹּאן,

דֶּבֶר כָּבֵד מְאֹד.

Q&A

Why is pestilence, of all the ten plagues, singled out as the example of the Hand of the Lord?

Pestilence is unusually singled out among the ten plagues as the example of the Hand of the Lord. Some commentators noted that pestilence was the fifth plague, and because each plague was likened to a finger, the fifth plague completed a full hand.

How can pestilence be likened to the Hand of the Lord when God is said to have redeemed the Israelites with a "mighty hand"?

Likening pestilence to the Hand of the Lord creates an apparent problem by analogy. The Torah teaches that God "brought us out of Egypt with a mighty hand". However, God did not bring us out of

"And an outstretched arm"

This [refers to] the sword.

As it is said:

"And His sword was drawn in His hand,

stretched out over Jerusalem."

---

days of pestilence. David chose three days of pestilence. Upon seeing an angel in the sky with a sword in his hand "stretched out over Jerusalem", that is, ready to deliver the pestilence, David pleaded for God's mercy. The sages who included this passage in the *Haggadah* may have seen a link between the plague of pestilence, and a punishment for wrongdoing to be meted out on David's kingdom through pestilence. Both "*zeroah netuyah*" (an outstretched arm) and "*shlufah netuyah*" (a sword stretched out") share the same word "*netuyah*". Nothing is coincidental in hermeneutics!

"And with great awe"

This [refers to] the revelation of the "Shechina".

As it is said:

"Has a god ever tried to come

to take for himself

a nation out of the midst of [another] nation,

with trials, with signs, and with wonders, and with war,

and with a strong hand, and an outstretched arm,

and with great deeds,

like all that the Lord, your God, did in Egypt before your eyes?"

---

appropriation". For much of its history, ancient Israel lived in the shadow of Egypt, the greatest power of the Near East. Professor Berman believes that the Torah explicitly appropriates this peculiar Egyptian phrase, "with a strong hand and an outstretched arm", as if to demonstrate in words the strength of the subservient power – Israel – over the dominant one – Egypt. This message perfectly coincides with one of the great messages of the story of the Exodus, one that has resonated throughout history. As the Prophet Elijah said, God is not found "in the wind . . . nor in the earthquake . . . but in a still, small voice". The ultimate significance of the strong hand and the outstretched arm is not the power of the great, visible miracles, but in the smallest, most surprising one. God did not protect Egypt, the greatest empire of the ancient world, rather He saved the lowly slaves, the Jewish people.

וּבִזְרֹעַ נְטוּיָה–

זוֹ הַחֶרֶב.
כְּמָה שֶׁנֶּאֱמַר:
וְחַרְבּוֹ שְׁלוּפָה בְּיָדוֹ,
נְטוּיָה עַל יְרוּשָׁלָיִם.

Q&A

How is God's sword drawn over Jerusalem refer to an outstretched arm?

The connection between "an outstretched arm" and a "sword . . . stretched out" is a fascinating example of classical Jewish hermeneutics. The passage comes from the first book of Chronicles, which describes a census that King David ordered be taken of the kingdom. God did not approve of this, as counting Jews is considered a sin (while God counted the Israelites in the desert following the Exodus, it was done as a way to raise money for the building of the *Mishkan*). God offered David a choice of three punishments, either three years of famine, three months of destruction by enemies, or three

---

וּבְמֹרָא גָּדֹל–

זוֹ גִּלּוּי שְׁכִינָה.
כְּמָה שֶׁנֶּאֱמַר:
אוֹ הֲנִסָּה אֱלֹהִים לָבוֹא
לָקַחַת לוֹ
גוֹי מִקֶּרֶב גּוֹי,
בְּמַסֹּת בְּאֹתֹת וּבְמוֹפְתִים וּבְמִלְחָמָה,
וּבְיָד חֲזָקָה וּבִזְרוֹעַ נְטוּיָה,
וּבְמוֹרָאִים גְּדֹלִים,
כְּכֹל אֲשֶׁר עָשָׂה לָכֶם יְהוָה אֱלֹהֵיכֶם בְּמִצְרַיִם לְעֵינֶיךָ?

Q&A

What significance is there to the phrase "a strong hand and an outstretched arm"?

With a strong hand and an outstretched arm" ("*b'yad chazakah u've'zeroah netuyah*") is a well-known phrase that the Torah uses several times to describe God acting on behalf of the Israelites. As explained by Professor Joshua Berman, professor of Bible at Bar Ilan University, it is a phrase that is only used in connection with the events of the Exodus. It is never used to describe any other of God's miracles, neither the conquest of the land of Canaan, nor the defeat of the Israelites' other enemies, nor any other occasion of redemption. In fact, the term is not used in any other Near Eastern literature or culture, except one. The phrase is only found in Egyptian royal propaganda inscriptions from the latter part of the second millennium BCE – the very time that the Exodus occurred. In Egyptian culture, the "strong hand" is a metaphor used to describe Pharaoh, and the "outstretched arm" as a metaphor for the manifestation of his power. Professor Berman argues that the Torah's use of the phrase suggests a type of "cultural is translated in Targum (the Aramaic translation of the Torah). As the *Shechinah* is the manifestation of God's earthly presence, then witnessing that manifestation in the various trials, signs and wonders that God performed on behalf of the Jewish people certainly would have caused a feeling of awe.

Why was it necessary for the *Shechinah* to be revealed?

After centuries of life in Egypt, first in comfort in the land of Goshen, and then under the yolk of slavery, the Israelites had become steeped in Egyptian culture. Undoubtedly, they lacked faith in God, and, as discussed in the *Haggadah*, were without *mitzvot*. How can such a people be taken out, not just from physical slavery, but from spiritual slavery? The Ramban, a 13th century Spanish commentator, said that miracles – public displays of phenomena that contravene the "way of the world and its nature" – occur to disprove heretical ideas, such as not believing in the existence of God or not believing in His omniscience or providence. Miracles, like the trials, signs and wonders that God displayed throughout the story of the Exodus, were needed to arouse the faith of the Israelites. The Malbim, a Polish rabbi of the 19th century, stated that only through the revelation of the *Shechinah* would the Israelites have abandoned the evil habits they had learned in Egypt.

"And with signs"

This [refers to] the staff.

As it is said:

"And this staff, take it in your hand,

and with it you shall perform the signs."

"And with wonders"

This [refers to] the blood.

As it is said:

"I shall make wonders

in the sky and on the earth:

A drop of wine is spilled from the cup as each wonder is mentioned:

"Blood, and Fire, and Pillars of Smoke."

What is the "*Shechinah*"?

The *Shechinah* is the manifestation of God's presence on earth. It is derived from the word "*shochen*", which means "to dwell within". Following the sin of the golden calf, God instructed Moses to tell the Israelites to make Him a *Mikdash*, or sanctuary, "*v'shachanti b'tocham*" ("so I may dwell within their midst"). The *Shechinah* is therefore closely connected with the *Mikdash*, which was built as a home for God's earthly presence. Although God is transcendent, the *Shechinah* is the expression of His imminence. Because the *Shechinah* is a feminine gendered word, it is also associated with the feminine aspect of God's nature. In kabbalistic thought, the *Shechinah* is portrayed as a loving mother. The kabbalists envisioned that while the Israelites toiled in slavery, they did not do so alone. They were always under the protection of the *Shechinah*.

Why does "great awe" refer to the *Shechinah*?

The word for "awe", "*morah*", shares common root letters – *resh–aleph–hey* – with the word "see", "*ro'eh*". Rashi, the medieval French commentator, saw in this a connection between "awe" and the *Shechinah*. Rather than "awe", "*morah*" could be translated as "witnessing" or "seeing", which is in fact how the word

---

וּבְאֹתוֹת –

זֶה הַמַּטֶּה.

כְּמָה שֶׁנֶּאֱמַר:

וְאֶת הַמַּטֶּה הַזֶּה תִּקַּח בְּיָדֶךָ,

אֲשֶׁר תַּעֲשֶׂה בּוֹ אֶת הָאֹתֹת.

וּבְמֹפְתִים –

זֶה הַדָּם.

כְּמָה שֶׁנֶּאֱמַר:

וְנָתַתִּי מוֹפְתִים

בַּשָּׁמַיִם וּבָאָרֶץ:

A drop of wine is spilled from the cup as each wonder is mentioned:

דָּם וָאֵשׁ וְתִימְרוֹת עָשָׁן.

that God will display at the end of times? Yoel declares that one of the three wonders will be "blood." What blood though is displayed in the Exodus? While many commentators opined that the "blood" referred to in this passage is the first plague, when the water of the Nile transformed into blood, that is problematic since we have learned that "signs and wonders" cannot be metaphors for the plagues. Other commentators, however, noted another display of blood in the story of the Exodus. God commanded Moses to go before Pharaoh, take water from the Nile and spill it on dry land, where it would become blood. However, before doing so, Moses is commanded to display "two signs". The first sign was the transformation of Moses' staff into a serpent and, the second, Moses' hand turning leprous. If these two lesser "signs" failed to convince Pharaoh, Moses was commanded to display the greater "wonder": the transformation of the Nile water into blood. This hermeneutic analysis then comes full circle. It demonstrates that the signs must be less convincing than the display of blood, which, because of the reference in the book of Yoel, must be a wonder!

What is the significance of "blood, fire and pillars of smoke" in the context of the Exodus?

We have just learned that God brought us out of Egypt "with signs and wonders", with the meaning of "wonders" derived from the Book of Yoel. Yoel spoke of the end of days, of the time just before the Messiah will come, when God "will perform wonders in the heavens and on the earth". What will those wonders be? Yoel states that they are "blood, fire and pillars of smoke". In pointing to this proof text, the rabbis are suggesting that our ultimate redemption, in the times of the Messiah, will come about in the same dramatic fashion as the Exodus. And just as our ancestors were redeemed, we should have faith that we too will be redeemed, as Yoel prophesied.

Another interpretation [of the passage "And the Lord brought us out from Egypt"]:

"With a strong hand" – [refers to] two [plagues].

"And with an outstretched arm" – [refers to] two [plagues].

"And with great awe" – [refers to] two [plagues].

"With signs" – [refers to] two [plagues].

"And with wonders" – [refers to] two [plagues].

---

plural, suggesting each corresponds to two plagues. The three preceding words, "hand", "arm" and "awe" are in the singular, but are each modified by an adjective, "strong", "outstretched" and "great", suggesting to the sages that each corresponds to two plagues. The five words therefore can be seen as referring to two plagues each, making ten plagues total.

Q&A

Why are "signs and wonders" not considered metaphors for all the plagues?

On their face, "signs and wonders" seem to refer to the plagues generally. However, the sages have traditionally considered that the repetition of words, as well as the use of a series of synonyms, must refer to separate and distinct ideas. Therefore, each of "signs" and "wonders" must refer to distinct things, otherwise these words would be superfluous, which is considered unacceptable by the sages. In this case, the sages saw in the word "signs" an allusion to Moses' staff, which was the instrument used to implement the signs.

How can Moses' staff be a "sign"?

A plain reading of the story of the Exodus seems to make Moses' staff nothing more than an instrument used by Moses when making his prophesies to Pharaoh of the upcoming plagues. However, the Ramban commented that a prophesy is normally accompanied by some physical act, which actualizes it. A sign is nothing more than a physical representation of a theoretical idea. In this way, Moses' staff served to take the theoretical possibility of each plague and transform it into material form.

How is blood a "wonder"?

While "signs" has a ready meaning derived from an unequivocal verse ("and this staff, take it . . . and with it . . . perform the signs"), the verse quoted to explicate "wonders" requires more imagination. The sages noted that "signs" and "wonders" are used here together. Abarbanel argued that while they are similar, both being miraculous displays of divine power, a "wonder" is of greater power than a "sign". A sign may be unconvincing, but a wonder is undeniable. Proof of this comes from the book of Yoel, which the *Haggadah* quotes here, "I shall make wonders in the sky and on the earth." What are these wonders

דָּבָר אַחֵר:

בְּיָד חֲזָקָה- שְׁתַּיִם,
וּבִזְרֹעַ נְטוּיָה- שְׁתַּיִם,
וּבְמֹרָא גָּדֹל- שְׁתַּיִם,
וּבְאֹתוֹת- שְׁתַּיִם,
וּבְמֹפְתִים- שְׁתַּיִם.

Q&A

How do each of these correspond to two plagues?

We are about to recite the Ten Plagues, which precipitated the Israelites redemption from Egypt. Yet, we have just read that God brought the Israelites out "with a strong hand and with an outstretched arm, with great awe, and with signs and wonders." That sounds like five things, not ten. The sages did not like any numeric contradictions. So, the Haggadah provides a reconciliation. "Signs" and "wonders" are in the

Spill a drop of wine either directly from the wine cup, or using a finger, as each plague, and each acronym Detzach, Adash and Be'achav, is mentioned.

For a transliteration of the Hebrew text, please turn to page 170.

These were the Ten Plagues

that the Holy One, blessed is He, brought upon the Egyptians in Egypt, and these are them:

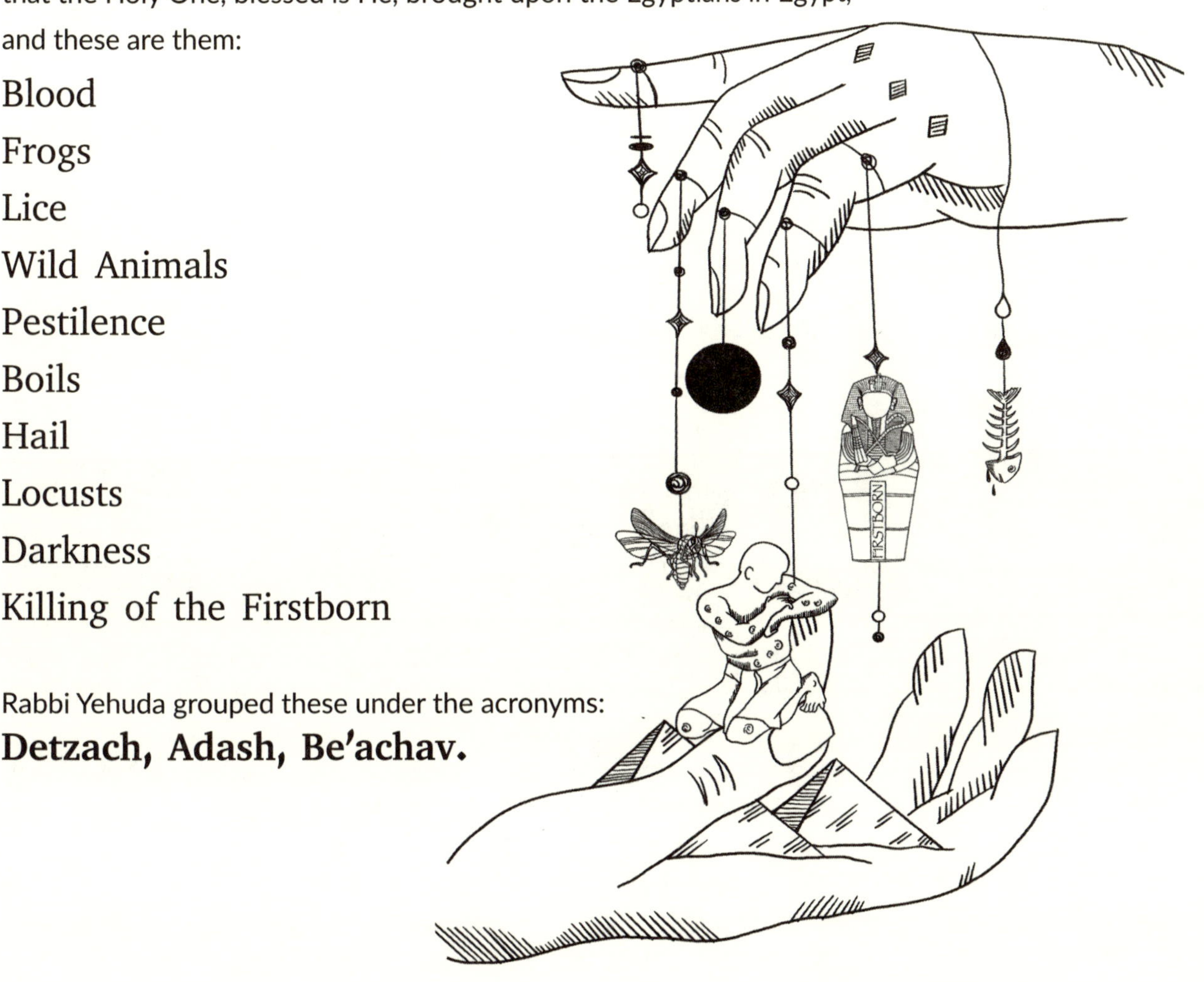

Blood

Frogs

Lice

Wild Animals

Pestilence

Boils

Hail

Locusts

Darkness

Killing of the Firstborn

Rabbi Yehuda grouped these under the acronyms:

Detzach, Adash, Be'achav.

Egyptian gods, just as all pagan gods, were seen as impersonal and as arbitrary actors. The plagues were meant to refute this Egyptian worldview. Behind the elements of nature are not many gods, but in fact one God who created and rules the entire world. Rather than punishing the Egyptians, the plagues can be seen as a dramatic lesson to teach them this truth.

How were the ten plagues miracles?

Many biblical scholars have attempted to reconcile the ten plagues with a modern, scientific worldview. According to this type of thinking, none of the plagues were miracles, as each one can be explained naturally. For example, the Nile can turn red from a certain type of algae growth, while swarms of frogs, lice and insects also can follow from the annual flooding of the Nile. The darkness could have been caused by sandstorms. None of the plagues would have been seen as unusual in Egypt. However, whether any individual plague was a "miracle", taken together, they were miraculous. These otherwise

Spill a drop of wine either directly from the wine cup, or using a finger, as each plague, and each acronym דצ"ך, עד"ש and באח"ב, is mentioned.

For a transliteration of the following text, please turn to page 170.

אֵלּוּ עֶשֶׂר מַכּוֹת

שֶׁהֵבִיא הַקָּדוֹשׁ בָּרוּךְ הוּא עַל הַמִּצְרִים בְּמִצְרַיִם,

וְאֵלּוּ הֵן:

דָּם

צְפַרְדֵּעַ

כִּנִּים

עָרוֹב

דֶּבֶר

שְׁחִין

בָּרָד

אַרְבֶּה

חֹשֶׁךְ

מַכַּת בְּכוֹרוֹת

רַבִּי יְהוּדָה הָיָה נוֹתֵן בָּהֶם סִימָנִים:

דְּצַ"ךְ עֲדַ"שׁ בְּאַחַ"ב.

Q&A

Why do we spill wine out after saying each plague?

Unlike other holidays, Passover is not described using the word "*simcha*" (rejoicing). While it is a time in which the Jewish people gained redemption from slavery, the Egyptians suffered as a result. We must give thanks to God for His kindness to us, but we also should reflect on the pain of others. In fact, this theme arises again during the story of the splitting of the sea, as related in the Talmud. When the sea split and the Egyptians were drowned, angels wished to sing a song of praise, but God silenced them saying, "My creatures are drowning in the sea, and you wish to sing a song?" Just as God did not rejoice in the downfall of the Egyptians, neither should we.

What is the overall message of the plagues?

The Egyptians, like all pagans of the ancient world, worshipped nature and the many gods that they viewed as controlling and personifying nature. Nature often seemed chaotic to people of that time. The

the Nile, which was believed to be the source of all life, and Khnum was also seen as a god of fertility and the fashioner of mankind. In order to save their firstborn, the Israelites were not only called upon to symbolically kill this god through the sacrifice of the lamb, but to do so in the light of the full moon on the night of the 14th of Nisan. This very public display of sacrifice and blood – in full view of the Egyptians – demonstrated their faith in God and acceptance of His sovereignty.

How was the killing of the firstborn a fitting punishment for the Egyptians?

The story of the Exodus begins in part with Pharaoh's command to kill all Jewish boys. On the simplest level, the final plague of the killing of the firstborn is a fitting, measure-for-measure punishment. However, on a deeper level, the tenth plague can be seen as the final act in the divine lesson to the Egyptians. As with all the plagues, the killing of the firstborn struck at the Egyptian's naturalistic worldview. According to the Egyptians, nature was worthy of worship. Birth order is itself a product of the randomness of nature. Thus, in most societies founded upon a naturalistic worldview, the firstborn represents the top of the natural hierarchy. The law of primogeniture, which states that the firstborn is entitled to the right of succession and to the entire or a super-inheritance, is rooted in this idea. Yet, as the birthright stories of the Torah teach, being born first does not mean being born to a superior birthright. The later born in fact is always preferred in the Biblical stories: Abel over Cain, Isaac over Yishmael, Jacob over Esau, Judah over Reuven, Ephraim over Menashe, and many others. To automatically prefer the firstborn is to give primacy to nature. Striking down the firstborn symbolically overthrows this system. The Egyptians would have seen themselves in regard to the Hebrews as the firstborn, the chosen people of their gods. By striking down the firstborn throughout Egypt, but sparing the Israelite firstborn, God demonstrated not only His might over the Egyptian gods, but also demonstrated who He considered to be his chosen firstborn, regardless of any naturalistic worldview.

How did Rabbi Yehuda group the plagues into the three acronyms?

Other than the killing of the firstborn, the plagues happened in groups of three, with each group sharing two common elements. The first three were preceded by a warning "in the morning" and then performed by Aaron. The second three were preceded by a warning without a specific time as to when they would occur, and then were performed by Moses. The last three were performed by Moses "stretching out his hand" without any warning.

Rabbi Yossei the Galilean says,

How do you know that the Egyptians were struck with ten plagues in Egypt

and were struck with fifty at the sea?

For in Egypt, what does it say?

"The astrologers said to Pharaoh, 'This is the finger of God'".

And at the sea, what does it say?

"When Israel saw the great hand the Lord raised against the Egyptians,

the people feared the Lord, and they believed in the Lord and in His servant Moses."

How many [plagues] were they struck with the finger? Ten plagues.

Conclude from this that they were struck with ten plagues in Egypt

and at the sea they were struck with fifty plagues.

natural events occurred not only according to the predictions of Moses, but at the precise times that they were needed to cause Pharaoh to free the Jewish people. This demonstrates that the ten plagues were indeed miracles, and evidence of God's providence in the world.

What is the significance of the Nile turning to blood? How might it relate to the last plague, the killing of the firstborn?

While many surrounding countries, like the land of Israel relied on unpredictable rainfall, the Nile river's annual flooding predictably replenished and enriched the soil, allowing Egypt to become the "breadbasket" of the ancient Near East. For the Egyptians, the Nile was no mere river, but the source of all life. The Egyptians believed that their god, Hapi, caused the Nile to flood, thereby providing the rich soil for growing crops. The first plague of blood was therefore a symbolic killing of Hapi. The plague of blood also recalls the last plague, the killing of the firstborn.

What is the significance of the plague of darkness?

Many of the plagues are symbolic acts of judgment against the gods of Egypt. The head of the Egyptian pantheon – the chief god – was Ra, the god of the sun. By blotting out all light, God demonstrated His mastery not only over nature itself, but symbolically over the god the Egyptians most revered.

How did the killing of the firstborn differ from all the other plagues?

The killing of the firstborn was unique among the ten plagues because it was the only plague that required the Israelites to do something. The Israelites were silent witnesses to the first nine plagues, and either there was no indication that they were harmed, or there was an affirmative statement that they were not. For example, the fifth plague of pestilence, which killed the animals, did not harm those owned by the Israelites, and the ninth plague of darkness, which blotted out all light, did not affect the Israelites in their homes. Only with the tenth plague were the Israelites commanded to protect themselves, implicitly indicating that failure to do so would result in the death of their firstborn as well. The Israelites were commanded to sacrifice a lamb, taken from their flocks of sheep or goats, and to put its blood on the doorposts. Those who marked their doorposts were spared. Those who did not mark their doorposts were not. This was far from a trivial act. The lamb was sacred to the Egyptians, who worshipped a god, Khnum, with the head of a goat or ram. Khunm was the god of the source of

---

רַבִּי יוֹסֵי הַגְּלִילִי אוֹמֵר:
מִנַּיִן אַתָּה אוֹמֵר שֶׁלָּקוּ הַמִּצְרִים בְּמִצְרַיִם עֶשֶׂר מַכּוֹת
וְעַל הַיָּם לָקוּ חֲמִשִּׁים מַכּוֹת?
בְּמִצְרַיִם מָה הוּא אוֹמֵר?
וַיֹּאמְרוּ הַחַרְטֻמִּם אֶל פַּרְעֹה אֶצְבַּע אֱלֹהִים הִוא.
וְעַל הַיָּם מָה הוּא אוֹמֵר?
וַיַּרְא יִשְׂרָאֵל אֶת הַיָּד הַגְּדֹלָה אֲשֶׁר עָשָׂה יְהֹוָה בְּמִצְרַיִם,
וַיִּירְאוּ הָעָם אֶת יְהֹוָה, וַיַּאֲמִינוּ בַּיהֹוָה וּבְמֹשֶׁה עַבְדּוֹ.
כַּמָּה לָקוּ בְּאֶצְבַּע? עֶשֶׂר מַכּוֹת.
אֱמֹר מֵעַתָּה: בְּמִצְרַיִם לָקוּ עֶשֶׂר מַכּוֹת
וְעַל הַיָּם לָקוּ חֲמִשִּׁים מַכּוֹת.

Rabbi Eliezer says,

How can you know that each and every plague
the Holy One, blessed is He, brought upon the Egyptians in Egypt
was [in fact] made up of four plagues?
As it is said, "His fury was sent down upon them, great anger, rage, and distress,
a company of messengers of destruction."
Great anger is one, and rage is two, and distress is three,
a company of messengers of destruction is four.
Conclude from this that they were struck with forty plagues in Egypt
and at the sea they were struck with two hundred plagues.

Rabbi Akiva says,

How can you know that each and every plague
that the Holy One, blessed is He, brought upon the Egyptians in Egypt
was [in fact] made up of five plagues?
As it is said, "His fury was sent down upon them, great anger, rage, and distress,
a company of messengers of destruction."
His fury is one, great anger is two, and rage is three,
and distress is four, a company of messengers of destruction is five.
Conclude from this that they were struck with fifty plagues in Egypt
and at the sea they were struck with two hundred and fifty plagues.

What is the meaning of this debate?

These rabbis were not simply arguing over how many plagues there were. Rather, the rabbis were discussing how much greater the miracle at the sea was than all the plagues. The plagues themselves appeared to be natural events, even if they occurred in a sequence and with a timing that showed their divine origin. By describing the miracle at the sea as the "hand of the Lord", this indicates how much greater that miracle was than the plagues, which were compared only to God's "finger". People who witnessed the plagues may have doubted their divine origin, but no one who was present at the splitting of the sea, the Jewish people walking on dry land between the walls of water, or the subsequent drowning of the Egyptians, could deny that this was a great miracle.

רַבִּי אֱלִיעֶזֶר אוֹמֵר:
מִנַּיִן שֶׁכָּל מַכָּה וּמַכָּה
שֶׁהֵבִיא הַקָּדוֹשׁ בָּרוּךְ הוּא עַל הַמִּצְרִים בְּמִצְרַיִם
הָיְתָה שֶׁל אַרְבַּע מַכּוֹת?
שֶׁנֶּאֱמַר: יְשַׁלַּח בָּם חֲרוֹן אַפּוֹ, עֶבְרָה וָזַעַם וְצָרָה,
מִשְׁלַחַת מַלְאֲכֵי רָעִים.
עֶבְרָה– אַחַת, וָזַעַם– שְׁתַּיִם, וְצָרָה– שָׁלֹשׁ,
מִשְׁלַחַת מַלְאֲכֵי רָעִים– אַרְבַּע.
אֱמֹר מֵעַתָּה: בְּמִצְרַיִם לָקוּ אַרְבָּעִים מַכּוֹת
וְעַל הַיָּם לָקוּ מָאתַיִם מַכּוֹת.

רַבִּי עֲקִיבָא אוֹמֵר:
מִנַּיִן שֶׁכָּל מַכָּה וּמַכָּה
שֶׁהֵבִיא הַקָּדוֹשׁ בָּרוּךְ הוּא עַל הַמִּצְרִים בְּמִצְרַיִם
הָיְתָה שֶׁל חָמֵשׁ מַכּוֹת?
שֶׁנֶּאֱמַר: יְשַׁלַּח בָּם חֲרוֹן אַפּוֹ, עֶבְרָה וָזַעַם וְצָרָה,
מִשְׁלַחַת מַלְאֲכֵי רָעִים.
חֲרוֹן אַפּוֹ– אַחַת, עֶבְרָה– שְׁתַּיִם, וָזַעַם– שָׁלֹשׁ,
וְצָרָה– אַרְבַּע, מִשְׁלַחַת מַלְאֲכֵי רָעִים– חָמֵשׁ.
אֱמֹר מֵעַתָּה: בְּמִצְרַיִם לָקוּ חֲמִשִּׁים מַכּוֹת
וְעַל הַיָּם לָקוּ חֲמִשִּׁים וּמָאתַיִם מַכּוֹת.

Q&A

Why is this debate included in the *Haggadah*?

At the beginning of the *Magid* section, we read that Rabbi Eliezer, Rabbi Yehoshua, Rabbi Elazar ben Azaria, Rabbi Akiva, and Rabbi Tarfon were up all night discussing the Exodus from Egypt. This text provides an example of the kind of discussions they had. They were interested in every single aspect of the story and would expound the meaning of every word. This debate is meant to encourage us to emulate them and to spend time discussing in detail the story of the Exodus. Moreover, it teaches us that Torah study must be a part of any important event.

How many levels of goodness did the Omnipresent bestow upon us!

If He had brought us out of Egypt,
but had not brought judgment upon them (the Egyptians), [it would have been] enough for us!

If He had brought judgment upon them,
but had not brought judgment upon their gods, [it would have been] enough for us!

If He had brought judgment upon their gods,
but had not killed their firstborn, [it would have been] enough for us!

If He had killed their firstborn,
but had not given us their wealth, [it would have been] enough for us!

If He had given us their wealth,
but had not split the sea for us, [it would have been] enough for us!

If He had split the sea for us,
but had not taken us through on dry land, [it would have been] enough for us!

If He had taken us through on dry land,
but had not drowned our enemies in the sea, [it would have been] enough for us!

If He had drowned our enemies in the sea,
but had not provided our needs in the desert for forty years, [it would have been] enough for us!

If He had provided our needs in the desert for forty years,
but had not fed us the manna, [it would have been] enough for us!

If He had fed us the manna,
but had not given us the Shabbat, [it would have been] enough for us!

If He had given us the Shabbat,
but had not brought us before Mount Sinai, [it would have been] enough for us!

כַּמָּה מַעֲלוֹת טוֹבוֹת לַמָּקוֹם עָלֵינוּ.

אִלּוּ הוֹצִיאָנוּ מִמִּצְרַיִם,
וְלֹא עָשָׂה בָהֶם שְׁפָטִים, דַּיֵּנוּ.

אִלּוּ עָשָׂה בָהֶם שְׁפָטִים,
וְלֹא עָשָׂה בֵאלֹהֵיהֶם, דַּיֵּנוּ.

אִלּוּ עָשָׂה בֵאלֹהֵיהֶם,
וְלֹא הָרַג אֶת בְּכוֹרֵיהֶם, דַּיֵּנוּ.

אִלּוּ הָרַג אֶת בְּכוֹרֵיהֶם,
וְלֹא נָתַן לָנוּ אֶת מָמוֹנָם, דַּיֵּנוּ.

אִלּוּ נָתַן לָנוּ אֶת מָמוֹנָם,
וְלֹא קָרַע לָנוּ אֶת הַיָּם, דַּיֵּנוּ.

אִלּוּ קָרַע לָנוּ אֶת הַיָּם,
וְלֹא הֶעֱבִירָנוּ בְתוֹכוֹ בֶּחָרָבָה, דַּיֵּנוּ.

אִלּוּ הֶעֱבִירָנוּ בְתוֹכוֹ בֶּחָרָבָה,
וְלֹא שִׁקַּע צָרֵינוּ בְּתוֹכוֹ, דַּיֵּנוּ.

אִלּוּ שִׁקַּע צָרֵינוּ בְּתוֹכוֹ,
וְלֹא סִפֵּק צָרְכֵּנוּ בַּמִּדְבָּר אַרְבָּעִים שָׁנָה, דַּיֵּנוּ.

אִלּוּ סִפֵּק צָרְכֵּנוּ בַּמִּדְבָּר אַרְבָּעִים שָׁנָה,
וְלֹא הֶאֱכִילָנוּ אֶת הַמָּן, דַּיֵּנוּ.

אִלּוּ הֶאֱכִילָנוּ אֶת הַמָּן,
וְלֹא נָתַן לָנוּ אֶת הַשַּׁבָּת, דַּיֵּנוּ.

אִלּוּ נָתַן לָנוּ אֶת הַשַּׁבָּת,
וְלֹא קֵרְבָנוּ לִפְנֵי הַר סִינַי, דַּיֵּנוּ.

If He had brought us before Mount Sinai,
but had not given us the Torah, [it would have been] enough for us!

If He had given us the Torah,
but had not brought us into the Land of Israel, [it would have been] enough for us!

If He had brought us into the Land of Israel,
but had not built for us the Chosen House (the Temple), [it would have been] enough for us!

How much more so
is the good that is doubled and quadrupled
that the Omnipresent bestowed upon us!

That He brought us out of Egypt;
that He brought judgment upon them;
that He brought judgment upon their gods;
that He killed their firstborn;
that He gave us their wealth;
that He split the sea for us;
that He took us through on dry land;
that He drowned our enemies in the sea;
that He provided our needs in the desert for forty years;
that He fed us the Manna;
that He gave us the Shabbat;
that He brought us before Mount Sinai;
that He gave us the Torah
that He brought us into the Land of Israel;
that He built for us the Chosen House to atone for our sins.

---

previous rabbi to accentuate the magnitude of the miracle at the sea compared to the plagues. This section now comes to emphasize that we can list many more miracles that God bestowed upon us, with each level of goodness greater than the previous. This sequence of recognizing God's many miracles is setting the mood for the transition to *Hallel*, which shortly follows this section, where we will praise God further.

אִלּוּ קֵרְבָנוּ לִפְנֵי הַר סִינַי,
וְלֹא נָתַן לָנוּ אֶת הַתּוֹרָה, דַּיֵּנוּ.

אִלּוּ נָתַן לָנוּ אֶת הַתּוֹרָה,
וְלֹא הִכְנִיסָנוּ לְאֶרֶץ יִשְׂרָאֵל, דַּיֵּנוּ.

אִלּוּ הִכְנִיסָנוּ לְאֶרֶץ יִשְׂרָאֵל,
וְלֹא בָנָה לָנוּ אֶת בֵּית הַבְּחִירָה, דַּיֵּנוּ.

עַל אַחַת כַּמָּה וְכַמָּה
טוֹבָה כְפוּלָה וּמְכֻפֶּלֶת
לַמָּקוֹם עָלֵינוּ:

שֶׁהוֹצִיאָנוּ מִמִּצְרַיִם,
וְעָשָׂה בָהֶם שְׁפָטִים,
וְעָשָׂה בֵאלֹהֵיהֶם,
וְהָרַג אֶת בְּכוֹרֵיהֶם,
וְנָתַן לָנוּ אֶת מָמוֹנָם,
וְקָרַע לָנוּ אֶת הַיָּם,
וְהֶעֱבִירָנוּ בְתוֹכוֹ בֶּחָרָבָה,
וְשִׁקַּע צָרֵינוּ בְּתוֹכוֹ,
וְסִפֵּק צָרְכֵּנוּ בַּמִּדְבָּר אַרְבָּעִים שָׁנָה,
וְהֶאֱכִילָנוּ אֶת הַמָּן,
וְנָתַן לָנוּ אֶת הַשַּׁבָּת,
וְקֵרְבָנוּ לִפְנֵי הַר סִינַי,
וְנָתַן לָנוּ אֶת הַתּוֹרָה,
וְהִכְנִיסָנוּ לְאֶרֶץ יִשְׂרָאֵל,
וּבָנָה לָנוּ אֶת בֵּית הַבְּחִירָה לְכַפֵּר עַל כָּל עֲוֹנוֹתֵינוּ.

Q&A

Why does the statement "How many levels of goodness did the Omnipresent bestow upon us!" follow the debate among Rabbis Yossei the Galilean, Eliezer and Akiva?

The *Haggadah* moves logically from section to section, despite appearances sometimes. We have just read of a debate among Rabbi Yossei the Galilean, Rabbi Eliezer, and Rabbi Akiva, with each one-upping the

the Temple, so too each level of goodness leads successively to a higher level of goodness, and ultimately, to the final, 15th level of goodness, which is the Temple itself.

What is the connection between *Dayeinu* and the Israelite's complaints in the story of the Exodus?

The Israelites complain 14 times from the start of the story of the Exodus until they reach the Land of Israel (the first (in Exodus 5:21) being when the people complain that because of Moses, Pharaoh increased their burdens, and the last time (in Numbers 21:5) when the people complained they would die for lack of bread and water). The 15 stanzas of *Dayeinu* in which we praise God's goodness therefore can be seen as acts of repentance for each of the 14 complaints, with the 15th level of goodness a demonstration of God's extra goodness.

What is the connection between the Exodus and the building of the Temple?

All the stanzas of *Dayeinu* have a direct connection to the Exodus (such as the ones related to the events preceding or during the Exodus itself), or an indirect connection (such as those related to the events in the desert), but the building of the Temple does not take place until long after the Exodus. The connection between the Exodus and the Temple is that the building of the Temple is the only event in the *Tanach* that is specifically dated with reference to the Exodus. The book of Kings states that it was built in the 480th year after the Israelites left Egypt. In addition, the Song of the Sea, which the Israelites sang in celebration after crossing through the split sea, states that "You shall bring them and plant them on the mount of Your heritage, directed toward Your habitation, which You made, Lord; the sanctuary, Lord, [which] Your hands established." Thus, the building of the Temple can be seen as the final event of the Exodus itself and the ultimate goal for which the Jewish people were released from bondage.

Rabban Gamliel would say:

Anyone who does not say these three things on Passover,

has not fulfilled his obligations.

And these are:

Pesach, Matzah, and Bitter Herbs

Why is it a commandment to say these three things, when commandments normally require doing something?

Commandments are normally fulfilled by doing something, like wearing *tzitzit*, or performing a *brit*, but *Pesach* involves both a commandment to do and to say. There is a commandment to eat *matzah*, and a commandment to tell the story of the Exodus. What Rabban Gamliel was saying is that there is a connection between the saying and the doing: the story explains the food. The Torah states that if a child asks "What is this service you observe [in connection with the eating of the Passover offering]", a parent should explain by telling the story: "for He passed over the houses of the children of Israel in Egypt while He struck down the Egyptians." Other people eat festive meals on different occasions, but the Passover meal is more than just a festive meal, it is a reenactment of history. Other people connect with each other through sharing a meal, but the Jewish people connect to the past through the Passover meal. This sharing of the past ensures a continuation of a Jewish future.

How could each level of goodness have been "enough" by itself?

Some of the levels of goodness God bestowed on the Israelites do not seem by themselves to have been "enough". For example, splitting the Sea, without leading us through, or bringing us to Mount Sinai, without giving us the Torah. However, the Malbim suggests that the proper way to understand "it would have been enough for us" is that each level of goodness was enough for us to praise God. Another way of viewing each level of goodness is from the perspective of the Israelites, rather than our own. Looking back on the Exodus, we know about each event and how the story ends. Knowing the ending makes it hard to imagine what Jewish history would have been like without all the levels of goodness. Indeed, from our perch today, we can legitimately ask, what would have happened if our ancestors had only been brought out of Egypt? However, from the perspective of the Israelites, who witnessed and experienced the Exodus as it occurred, each level of goodness would have been enough. After centuries of slavery, simply being brought out of Egypt was enough. Then to have judgment brought on their oppressors! That too was enough. Then God brought judgment on the Egyptian gods! Again, that was enough from their perspective. Yet, God continually offered more and more levels of goodness, none of which could have been expected by our ancestors. If we are truly to see ourselves as having been brought out of Egypt, we can see exactly how each level of goodness by itself "would have been enough for us"!

What is the significance of the number fifteen in *Dayeinu*?

The most obvious significance of the number 15 in *Dayeinu* is the use of the word *ma'alot* ("levels") in the sentence that precedes *Dayeinu*. Just as there are 15 "levels" (*ma'alot*) of goodness that God bestowed upon us that are described in *Dayeinu*, there are also 15 psalms that begin with the phrase, "*Shir HaMa'alot*" (Song of Ascents). The 15 levels of goodness also allude to the 15 Temple steps that the Levites stood on as they sang praises to God. The Maharal of Prague, the leading Talmudist and kabbalist in the 16th century, brings both of these allusions together in noting that just as 15 steps lead upward to

---

רַבָּן גַּמְלִיאֵל הָיָה אוֹמֵר:
כָּל שֶׁלֹּא אָמַר שְׁלֹשָׁה דְבָרִים אֵלּוּ בַּפֶּסַח,
לֹא יָצָא יְדֵי חוֹבָתוֹ.
וְאֵלּוּ הֵן:

פֶּסַח, מַצָּה וּמָרוֹר

Q&A

Why does Rabban Gamliel's directive follow *Dayeinu*?

Despite what seems to be a convoluted textual progression, the *Haggadah* follows logically from section to section. Earlier we learned that the correct response to the Son Who Does Not Know How to Ask is "And you shall tell your child on that day, 'Because of this the Lord acted for me when I came out of Egypt.'" What is "this"? We learned from the subsequent section that we may only say "because of this" when *matzah* and bitter herbs are before us at the *seder* table. Yet, it would be easy for us to believe that we have fulfilled the obligation to tell our children of the Exodus after having read the many passages, which ultimately culminated in *Dayeinu*. Rabban Galmliel tells us explicitly that, no, we have not yet fulfilled our obligation. We must now partake of the *Pesach* [Passover offering], *matzah*, and the bitter herbs.

Why are these three – Pesach, *matzah* and bitter herbs - so important to the *seder*?

The commandment to eat the *Pesach* [Passover offering], *matzah* and bitter herbs comes directly from the Torah. In the book of Exodus, it states, "And on this night, they shall eat the meat [of the Passover offering], roasted over fire, and the unleavened bread [the *matzah*], with bitter herbs they shall eat it."

The Pesach [Passover offering] that our ancestors would eat while the Temple stood,
what does it recall?
It recalls the Holy One's passing over [Pesach] the houses of our ancestors in Egypt.
As it is said:
"You shall say: 'It is a Pesach [Passover offering] for the Lord,
for He passed over the houses of the children of Israel in Egypt
while He struck the Egyptians,
but saved those in our homes,
and the people bowed and prostrated themselves.' "

Lift the matzot and say:

This Matzah that we eat, what does it recall?
It recalls the dough of our ancestors, which did not have enough [time] to rise
before the King, King of Kings, was revealed to them,
[and] the Holy One, blessed is He, redeemed [them].
As it is said:
"They baked the dough that they had brought out of Egypt into unleavened cakes,
for it had not risen, for they were cast out of Egypt and could not delay,
and they made no provision for themselves."

Lift the bitter herbs and say:

These bitter herbs that we eat, what do they recall?
They recall the bitterness that the Egyptians imposed on the lives of our ancestors in Egypt.
As it is said:
"They embittered their lives with hard labor,
with clay and with bricks, and with all field labors,
all the work with which they enslaved them – was crushing [labor]."

Why do we not lift the roasted bone on the *seder* plate, as we do to the *matzah* and bitter herbs?

Unlike the *matzah* and the bitter herbs, the roasted bone is only a symbol, it is not in fact a Passover offering. The sages forbid raising up and pointing to the roasted bone, so that it would not be misinterpreted as being a sacrifice dedication.

פֶּסַח שֶׁהָיוּ אֲבוֹתֵינוּ אוֹכְלִים בִּזְמַן שֶׁבֵּית הַמִּקְדָּשׁ הָיָה קַיָּם,
עַל שׁוּם מָה?
עַל שׁוּם שֶׁפָּסַח הַקָּדוֹשׁ בָּרוּךְ הוּא עַל בָּתֵּי אֲבוֹתֵינוּ בְּמִצְרַיִם.
שֶׁנֶּאֱמַר:
וַאֲמַרְתֶּם זֶבַח פֶּסַח הוּא לַיהֹוָה,
אֲשֶׁר פָּסַח עַל בָּתֵּי בְנֵי יִשְׂרָאֵל בְּמִצְרַיִם
בְּנָגְפּוֹ אֶת מִצְרַיִם,
וְאֶת בָּתֵּינוּ הִצִּיל,
וַיִּקֹּד הָעָם וַיִּשְׁתַּחֲווּ.

Lift the מצות and say:

מַצָּה זוֹ שֶׁאָנוּ אוֹכְלִים, עַל שׁוּם מָה?
עַל שׁוּם שֶׁלֹּא הִסְפִּיק בְּצֵקָם שֶׁל אֲבוֹתֵינוּ לְהַחֲמִיץ
עַד שֶׁנִּגְלָה עֲלֵיהֶם מֶלֶךְ מַלְכֵי הַמְּלָכִים,
הַקָּדוֹשׁ בָּרוּךְ הוּא וּגְאָלָם.
שֶׁנֶּאֱמַר:
וַיֹּאפוּ אֶת הַבָּצֵק אֲשֶׁר הוֹצִיאוּ מִמִּצְרַיִם עֻגֹת מַצּוֹת
כִּי לֹא חָמֵץ, כִּי גֹרְשׁוּ מִמִּצְרַיִם וְלֹא יָכְלוּ לְהִתְמַהְמֵהַּ,
וְגַם צֵדָה לֹא עָשׂוּ לָהֶם.

Lift the מרור and say:

מָרוֹר זֶה שֶׁאָנוּ אוֹכְלִים, עַל שׁוּם מָה?
עַל שׁוּם שֶׁמֵּרְרוּ הַמִּצְרִים אֶת חַיֵּי אֲבוֹתֵינוּ בְּמִצְרַיִם.
שֶׁנֶּאֱמַר:
וַיְמָרֲרוּ אֶת חַיֵּיהֶם בַּעֲבֹדָה קָשָׁה,
בְּחֹמֶר וּבִלְבֵנִים וּבְכָל עֲבֹדָה בַּשָּׂדֶה,
אֵת כָּל עֲבֹדָתָם אֲשֶׁר עָבְדוּ בָהֶם בְּפָרֶךְ.

Q&A

What do these foods – Pesach, *matzah* and bitter herbs - symbolize?

The Passover offering symbolizes freedom. The blood of the lamb sacrificed in the offering was put on the doorposts of the Israelites' homes to protect against the plague of the killing of the firstborn, and it was in the merit of that offering that the Jewish people were redeemed to freedom. The bitter herbs, of course, symbolize slavery. Matzah symbolizes both slavery and freedom. Slavery, because Matzah is the bread of affliction, which the Jewish people ate during slavery, and the bread of freedom, because the Jewish people at it when they left Egypt.

In each generation,

each person must see himself as if he left Egypt.

As it is said:
"And you shall tell your child that day, saying:
'Because of this, the Lord acted for me when I came out of Egypt.'"
It was not only our ancestors whom the Holy One, blessed is He, redeemed,
but he redeemed us too with them.

As it is said:
"He took us out of there,
to bring us and to give us the land he promised our forefathers."

The Exodus shaped who we are. If God merely set the Jewish people free from slavery in Egypt, it would not be possible to see oneself as having personally left. However, as the text states, God redeemed us "to bring us and to give us the land He promised our ancestors". This is a multi-generational, even multi-millennial mission that connects every Jewish person to the Exodus itself. Seeing oneself as having personally left Egypt brings the opportunity for each Jew to feel personally connected to the entire Jewish people and to our shared mission every day.

What is the Chassidic "*mitzrayim*" and how does it relate to this commandment?

In Chassidic thought, the word for Egypt, "*mitzrayim*", is related to the word "narrow straits". *Mitzrayim* is seen not just as the physical place of Egypt, but a mystical place within each person. We are all shackled by our own spiritual limitations that feel like boundaries that separate us from our potential. Our ancestors departed the land of *Mitzrayim*, but they continued a physical journey through the desert that included forty-two encampments. Each encampment is thought of as another step in their spiritual journey. So too, we can liken our own spiritual journey as steps in a process to release ourselves from the "*mitzrayim*" that are holding us back. Ultimately, we can see that just as God was there to redeem our ancestors from a physical *Mitzrayim*, He is there to do the same for us in our personal, spiritual "*mitzrayim*."

בְּכָל דּוֹר וָדוֹר

חַיָּב אָדָם לִרְאוֹת אֶת עַצְמוֹ כְּאִלּוּ הוּא יָצָא מִמִּצְרַיִם.

שֶׁנֶּאֱמַר:
וְהִגַּדְתָּ לְבִנְךָ בַּיּוֹם הַהוּא לֵאמֹר,
בַּעֲבוּר זֶה עָשָׂה יְהֹוָה לִי בְּצֵאתִי מִמִּצְרָיִם.
לֹא אֶת אֲבוֹתֵינוּ בִּלְבַד גָּאַל הַקָּדוֹשׁ בָּרוּךְ הוּא,
אֶלָּא אַף אוֹתָנוּ גָּאַל עִמָּהֶם.

שֶׁנֶּאֱמַר:
וְאוֹתָנוּ הוֹצִיא מִשָּׁם,
לְמַעַן הָבִיא אֹתָנוּ לָתֶת לָנוּ אֶת הָאָרֶץ אֲשֶׁר נִשְׁבַּע לַאֲבֹתֵינוּ.

Q&A

Where does this commandment to see oneself as having left Egypt come from?

Tractate *Pesachim* of the Mishnah states that "each person must see himself as if he left Egypt...". This is derived from the commandment in the Book of Exodus: "And you shall tell your son on that day, saying: 'It is because of this which God did for me when I came out of Egypt.' "

Why does each person need to see himself as having left Egypt personally?

The Torah commands that a parent tell his son the story from the first-person perspective. The commandment does not say that a parent should tell his son, "It is because of this which God did for our ancestors when they came out of Egypt", it says "for me when I came out of Egypt".

How can this commandment be relevant not just on Passover, but every day?

The *Haggadah* gives us a direct answer to this question following the Four Questions when it states, "if the Holy One, blessed is He, had not brought our ancestors out of Egypt – then we, and our children, and our children's children, would still be enslaved to Pharaoh in Egypt." To be a Jew is not simply to be an individual or even part of a group, but a part of a people whose historic roots trace back thousands of years. We are connected to those who came before us, and could not stand in the present but for them.

Cover the matzot and raise the cup of wine.

Therefore,

It is our duty to thank, praise, laud, glorify,
exalt, honor, bless, raise high, and acclaim
the One who has performed all these miracles for our ancestors and for us;
who has brought us out from slavery to freedom, from sorrow to joy,
from grief to celebration, from darkness to great light,
and from enslavement to redemption.
And so, we shall say before Him a new song.
Halleluyah!

Why has the *Haggadah* switched from Magid to *Hallel*?

At this point in the *Haggadah*, participants may be tiring, and their attentions may be drifting off. Now is not the time to tune out! This is an important transition in the *Haggadah*. We have read, questioned, and discussed many aspects of the Jewish people's journey down to Egypt, our enslavement, suffering, and redemption. As Jews, this remembrance and reliving of our collective history helps to ensure the continuity of our communal life. However, throughout Jewish history important moments have called for the simple act of praise as well. From the praises of Moses and Miriam as they led the Jewish people in song at the splitting of the sea, to Deborah's song in praise of the defeat of the Canaanites, to the many songs of praise attributed to King David that have been part of Jewish Temple and synagogue practice, as well as of private prayer for thousands of years, praising is a cornerstone of Jewish life.

Put the cup of wine down.

Halleluyah, offer praise, servants of the Lord, praise the Name of the Lord.
May the Lord's Name be blessed from no until the end of time.
From the rising of the sun to its setting, the Lord's Name be praised.
The Lord is high above all nations, His glory is over the heavens.
Who is like the Lord, our God, who dwells on high,
yet looks down so low upon heaven and earth?
He raises the poor from the dust, He lifts the needy from the refuse heap,
to seat them with nobles, with the nobles of His people.
He restores the barren woman to the house, into a joyful mother of children.
Halleluyah!

Cover the מצות and raise the cup of wine.

לְפִיכָךְ,

אֲנַחְנוּ חַיָּבִים לְהוֹדוֹת, לְהַלֵּל, לְשַׁבֵּחַ, לְפָאֵר,
לְרוֹמֵם, לְהַדֵּר, לְבָרֵךְ, לְעַלֵּה וּלְקַלֵּס
לְמִי שֶׁעָשָׂה לַאֲבוֹתֵינוּ וְלָנוּ אֶת כָּל הַנִּסִּים הָאֵלּוּ,
הוֹצִיאָנוּ מֵעַבְדוּת לְחֵרוּת, מִיָּגוֹן לְשִׂמְחָה,
וּמֵאֵבֶל לְיוֹם טוֹב וּמֵאֲפֵלָה לְאוֹר גָּדוֹל,
וּמִשִּׁעְבּוּד לִגְאֻלָּה.
וְנֹאמַר לְפָנָיו שִׁירָה חֲדָשָׁה.
הַלְלוּיָהּ!

Q&A

What is *Hallel*?

"Hallel" means "praise". The *Hallel* is a group of Psalms that forms the main part of a special prayer of thanksgiving that is recited on *Rosh Chodesh, Pesach, Shavuot, Sukkot, Shemini Atzeret, Simchat Torah,* and *Chanukkah*. In modern times it is also recited on Israel's Independence Day and on Jerusalem Day. Because *Hallel* is recited in praise of great events and miracles, it should be sung. Singing is a particularly powerful way of demonstrating great joy. Even though "*simcha*" or joy is most obviously associated with Sukkot (as it is called the "time of our joy", *"zman simchateinu"*), *Hallel* is recited most often on *Pesach*. It is recited in full on the first two nights and days, in part on the last six days, and as part of the *seder* itself. Considering the miracles of the events related to *Pesach*, it is no wonder that we should sing so much praise for the miracles God bestowed on the Jewish people!

Put the cup of wine down.

הַלְלוּיָהּ הַלְלוּ עַבְדֵי יְהֹוָה הַלְלוּ אֶת שֵׁם יְהֹוָה.
יְהִי שֵׁם יְהֹוָה מְבֹרָךְ מֵעַתָּה וְעַד עוֹלָם.
מִמִּזְרַח שֶׁמֶשׁ עַד מְבוֹאוֹ מְהֻלָּל שֵׁם יְהֹוָה.
רָם עַל כָּל גּוֹיִם יְהֹוָה, עַל הַשָּׁמַיִם כְּבוֹדוֹ.
מִי כַּיהֹוָה אֱלֹהֵינוּ הַמַּגְבִּיהִי לָשָׁבֶת,
הַמַּשְׁפִּילִי לִרְאוֹת בַּשָּׁמַיִם וּבָאָרֶץ?
מְקִימִי מֵעָפָר דָּל, מֵאַשְׁפֹּת יָרִים אֶבְיוֹן,
לְהוֹשִׁיבִי עִם נְדִיבִים, עִם נְדִיבֵי עַמּוֹ.
מוֹשִׁיבִי עֲקֶרֶת הַבַּיִת, אֵם הַבָּנִים שְׂמֵחָה.
הַלְלוּיָהּ!

please turn to page 170.

When Israel went out of Egypt,
the House of Jacob from a people of a foreign language,
Judah became His holy one, Israel His dominion.
The sea saw and fled, the Jordan turned backward.
The mountains skipped like rams, the hills like lambs.
What happened to you, O' sea, that you fled; O' Jordan, that you turned backward?
O' mountains, that you skipped like rams; O' hills, like lambs?
It was in the presence of the Master, who created the earth,
it was in the presence of the God of Jacob,
who transforms the rock into a pond of water, the flint into a fountain of water.

Raise the cup of wine.

Blessed are You, Lord, our God, King of the universe,
who has redeemed us and redeemed our ancestors from Egypt,
and enabled us to attain this night to eat Matzah and Maror.
So too, Lord, our God and God of our forefathers,
enable us to attain future holidays and festivals
that will come to us in peace with happiness in the rebuilding of Your city,
and with rejoicing in Your service [in the rebuilt Temple].
Then we shall eat there of the sacrifices and of the Passover offerings
(On Saturday night say: of the Passover-offerings and of the sacrifices)
whose blood shall be sprinkled on the wall of Your altar for acceptance.
And we shall thank You with a new song for our redemption
and for the deliverance of our souls.
Blessed are You, Lord, who redeems Israel.

Recite the following blessing, and drink the cup in the reclining position:

Blessed are You, Lord, our God, King of the universe,
who creates the fruit of the vine.

For a transliteration of the following text, please turn to page 170.

בְּצֵאת יִשְׂרָאֵל מִמִּצְרָיִם,
בֵּית יַעֲקֹב מֵעַם לֹעֵז,
הָיְתָה יְהוּדָה לְקָדְשׁוֹ יִשְׂרָאֵל מַמְשְׁלוֹתָיו.
הַיָּם רָאָה וַיָּנֹס הַיַּרְדֵּן יִסֹּב לְאָחוֹר.
הֶהָרִים רָקְדוּ כְאֵילִים גְּבָעוֹת כִּבְנֵי צֹאן.
מַה לְּךָ הַיָּם כִּי תָנוּס, הַיַּרְדֵּן תִּסֹּב לְאָחוֹר?
הֶהָרִים תִּרְקְדוּ כְאֵילִים, גְּבָעוֹת כִּבְנֵי צֹאן?
מִלִּפְנֵי אָדוֹן חוּלִי אָרֶץ,
מִלִּפְנֵי אֱלוֹהַּ יַעֲקֹב,
הַהֹפְכִי הַצּוּר אֲגַם מָיִם, חַלָּמִישׁ לְמַעְיְנוֹ מָיִם.

Raise the cup of wine.

בָּרוּךְ אַתָּה יְהֹוָה אֱלֹהֵינוּ מֶלֶךְ הָעוֹלָם,
אֲשֶׁר גְּאָלָנוּ וְגָאַל אֶת אֲבוֹתֵינוּ מִמִּצְרַיִם,
וְהִגִּיעָנוּ הַלַּיְלָה הַזֶּה לֶאֱכָל בּוֹ מַצָּה וּמָרוֹר.
כֵּן יְהֹוָה אֱלֹהֵינוּ וֵאלֹהֵי אֲבוֹתֵינוּ,
יַגִּיעֵנוּ לְמוֹעֲדִים וְלִרְגָלִים אֲחֵרִים הַבָּאִים
לִקְרָאתֵנוּ לְשָׁלוֹם, שְׂמֵחִים בְּבִנְיַן עִירֶךָ,
וְשָׂשִׂים בַּעֲבוֹדָתֶךָ.
וְנֹאכַל שָׁם מִן הַזְּבָחִים וּמִן הַפְּסָחִים
(במוצאי שבת: מִן הַפְּסָחִים וּמִן הַזְּבָחִים)
אֲשֶׁר יַגִּיעַ דָּמָם עַל קִיר מִזְבַּחֲךָ לְרָצוֹן.
וְנוֹדֶה לְּךָ שִׁיר חָדָשׁ עַל גְּאֻלָּתֵנוּ
וְעַל פְּדוּת נַפְשֵׁנוּ.
בָּרוּךְ אַתָּה יְהֹוָה, גָּאַל יִשְׂרָאֵל.

Recite the following ברכה, and drink the cup in the reclining position:

בָּרוּךְ אַתָּה יְהֹוָה אֱלֹהֵינוּ מֶלֶךְ הָעוֹלָם,
בּוֹרֵא פְּרִי הַגָּפֶן.

RACHTZAH
HANDWASH WITH BLESSING

Wash hands and recite the following blessing:

Blessed are You, Lord, our God, King of the universe,
who has sanctified us with His commandments
and commanded us concerning taking up [washing] the hands.

Refrain from speaking until after making the next two blessings and eating the matzah.

MOTZI MATZAH
BLESSINGS OVER THE MATZAH

Take the matzot in the order that they are lying on the tray-
the broken piece between the two whole matzot;
hold them in your hand and recite the following blessing:

Blessed are You, Lord, our God, King of the universe,
who brings forth bread from the earth.

Do not break anything off the matzot. First put down the third matzah (the bottom one),
and recite the following blessing over the broken matzah and the top one.
When reciting the following blessing, keep in mind that it also refers to the eating of the Korech "Sandwich",
which will be made with the third matzah - and also the eating of the Afikoman.

Blessed are You, Lord, our God, King of the universe,
who has sanctified us with His commandments
and commanded us concerning the eating of Matzah.

Now break off a k'zayit (the volume of one olive, or approximately the size of two-thirds of a machine-made matzah)
of the two matzot held and eat the two pieces together while reclining.

---

blessing, however, concerns the commandment to eat *matzah* on Passover. Unlike when eating *matzah* at any other time, we must eat it at the seder. The second blessing acknowledges this obligation.

רחצה

Wash hands and recite the following ברכה:

בָּרוּךְ אַתָּה יְהֹוָה אֱלֹהֵינוּ מֶלֶךְ הָעוֹלָם,
אֲשֶׁר קִדְּשָׁנוּ בְּמִצְוֹתָיו
וְצִוָּנוּ עַל נְטִילַת יָדָיִם.

Refrain from speaking until after making the next two ברכות and eating the מצה.

מוציא מצה

Take the מצות in the order that they are lying on the tray-
the broken piece between the two whole מצות;
hold them in your hand and recite the following ברכה:

בָּרוּךְ אַתָּה יְהֹוָה אֱלֹהֵינוּ מֶלֶךְ הָעוֹלָם,
הַמּוֹצִיא לֶחֶם מִן הָאָרֶץ.

Do not break anything off the מצות. First put down the third מצה (the bottom one),
and recite the following blessing over the broken מצה and the top one.
When reciting the following ברכה, keep in mind that it also refers to the eating of the כורך,
which will be made with the third מצה - and also the eating of the אפיקומן.

בָּרוּךְ אַתָּה יְהֹוָה אֱלֹהֵינוּ מֶלֶךְ הָעוֹלָם,
אֲשֶׁר קִדְּשָׁנוּ בְּמִצְוֹתָיו
וְצִוָּנוּ עַל אֲכִילַת מַצָּה.

Now break off a כזית (the volume of one olive, or approximately the size of two-thirds of a machine-made מצה)
of the two מצות held and eat the two pieces together while reclining.

Q&A

Why do we say two blessings over the *matzah*?

We say two blessings over the *matzah* because eating *matzah* during the seder involves two separate actions. Even when eating *matzah* at any time during the year other than at the seder, *matzah* is considered a bread-product. We therefore need to say the *hamotzi* blessing before eating it. The second

MAROR

DIP THE MAROR IN CHAROSET

Take a k'zayit (the volume of one olive, or approximately the size of two-thirds of a machine-made matzah) of the maror, dip it into the charoset and recite the following blessing:

Blessed are You, Lord, our God, King of the universe,
who has sanctified us with His commandments
and commanded us concerning the eating of Maror.

Eat the maror without reclining.

What does the *maror* represent?

The *maror* represents the bitterness of slavery. As with all the symbolic foods, it is meant as a physical representation – one that we can literally taste – of the events surrounding the Exodus. However, originally the *maror* may have evoked freedom, rather than bitterness. When the Temple stood, the *maror* was eaten with roasted lamb, and may have been a seasoning for the meat. Roast lamb is something that only free people could enjoy. Slaves ate simple foods – like unleavened bread – not roast lamb, let alone roast lamb so finely seasoned!

Why do we eat the maror alone, if the commandment is to eat it with the Passover offering, which we cannot eat (because the Temple no longer stands)?

The commandment to eat the *maror* is found in the book of Numbers, "They shall eat it [the Passover offering] with unleavened bread [*matzah*] and bitter herbs". The sages state in the Talmud that the commandment to eat the bitter herbs is inseparable from eating the lamb, unlike eating the *matzah*, which is a separate commandment. Following the destruction of the Temple, the scriptural basis for eating the bitter herbs ended (as with much other Temple–related commandments), but the sages ordained that we should continue to eat the bitter herbs to evoke the memory of Temple times.

מרור

Take a כזית (the volume of one olive, or approximately the size of two-thirds of a machine-made מצה) of the מרור, dip it into the חרוסת and recite the following ברכה

בָּרוּךְ אַתָּה יְהֹוָה אֱלֹהֵינוּ מֶלֶךְ הָעוֹלָם,
אֲשֶׁר קִדְּשָׁנוּ בְּמִצְוֹתָיו
וְצִוָּנוּ עַל אֲכִילַת מָרוֹר.

Eat the מרור without reclining.

Why do we not say a blessing over the *maror*?

The blessing made here is over the commandment to eat the bitter herbs, rather than over the bitter herbs themselves. We have already made a blessing over the *karpas*, and this serves to cover the *maror* as well.

Which vegetable do we use as *maror*?

Customs differ over which vegetable to use as the *maror*. In Mishnaic times, lettuce (*chazeret*) was used. In Europe, where lettuce was difficult to get at the time of Pesach, horseradish was used. Today, many continue to use horseradish as *maror* when eaten by itself, but use romaine lettuce (*chazeret*) when eaten in the Hillel sandwich.

KORECH
HILLEL SANDWICH

Take at least a k'zayit of the third piece of matzah (approximately two-thirds of a piece of machine-made matzah), break in two, and place bitter herbs with charoset between them to form a sandwich. Say the following:

In the memory of the Temple, as Hillel [did].

Thus did Hillel do in the time that the Temple existed:

He would combine Pesach, Matzah and Maror and eat them together

to fulfill what is said:

"They shall eat it with Matzah and bitter herbs."

Eat the matzah and bitter herbs together in a reclining position.

What does the *korech* sandwich represent?

The *korech* sandwich is a union of two opposites. While the *matzah* represents freedom, the *maror* represents the bitterness of slavery. Although other sages believed that they should be eaten separately, Rabbi Hillel believed they should be eaten together. We can learn from this that even though we are now free, we must not lose the memory of what it means to be slaves. This is a fundamental lesson of Judaism. We may live in the present, but we must never forget our past.

כורך

Take at least a כזית of the third piece of מצה (approximately two-thirds of a piece of machine-made מצה), break in two, and place מרור with חרוסת between them to form a sandwich. Say the following:

זֵכֶר לְמִקְדָּשׁ כְּהִלֵּל.
כֵּן עָשָׂה הִלֵּל בִּזְמַן שֶׁבֵּית הַמִּקְדָּשׁ הָיָה קַיָּם:
הָיָה כּוֹרֵךְ פֶּסַח, מַצָּה וּמָרוֹר וְאוֹכֵל בְּיַחַד
לְקַיֵּם מָה שֶׁנֶּאֱמַר:
עַל מַצּוֹת וּמְרֹרִים יֹאכְלֻהוּ.

Eat the מצה and מרור together in a reclining position.

Q&A

What vegetable should we use as bitter herbs in the *korech* sandwich?

When romaine lettuce is unavailable, as it was in previous times, it is acceptable to use the *maror* (horseradish) as the bitter herbs. When available though it is preferable to use *chazeret* (romaine lettuce). Some have the custom of using romaine lettuce and horseradish together.

Why do we eat the *korech* sandwich?

The *korech* sandwich reminds us of the commandment to eat the Passover offering, *matzah* and bitter herbs together. Although we are unable to eat the Passover offering, because the Temple is no longer standing, the sages commanded us to continue to eat the bitter herbs in order that we may recall the Temple. That is why the words of Rabbi Hillel, one of the greatest sages of the Temple period, are quoted here.

Why do we not say a blessing over the *korech* sandwich?

The reason we do not say a blessing over the *korech* sandwich is that there is no commandment to eat it and we have already said a blessing over each of the *matzah* and the *karpas*, which covers the bitter herbs as well.

SHULCHAN ORECH

THE FESTIVE MEAL

Eat the festive meal. Drinking wine is permitted.

TZAFUN

EATING THE AFIKOMAN

Following the festive meal, if children are present, they should search for the remaining piece of the middle matzah (the Afikoman), which was hidden earlier. Distribute the Afikoman among the guests. Eat it while reclining. Traditionally, it is prohibited to eat or drink (other than water) after eating the Afikoman.

שולחן עורך

Eat the festive meal. Drinking wine is permitted.

צפון

Following the festive meal, if children are present, they should search for the remaining piece of the middle מצה (the אפיקומן), which was hidden earlier. Distribute the אפיקומן among the guests. Eat it while reclining. Traditionally, it is prohibited to eat or drink (other than water) after eating the אפיקומן.

What does "Afikoman" mean?

"Afikoman" is not a Hebrew or Aramaic word. While its origin is in some dispute, it almost certainly is a Greek word. It may mean the last item eaten at a meal (the "dessert"), or it may mean "a drinking party". In either case, the sages who developed the *seder* were aware of the Greek custom for ending their symposiums (lively gatherings for discussions and debates among noble and elite guests) with drunken revelry. The Jewish sages frowned upon this type of behavior, but at the same time saw in the symposium something to emulate. As with other aspects of the classical symposium, the sages borrowed what they liked and refashioned the symposium into something distinctly Jewish. In contrast to the Greeks, who ended a symposium with more food and drinks (and some say other hedonistic pleasures), the sages forbade eating and drinking after eating the *Afikoman*. The sages took something that was seen as profane, and made it holy.

What does "tzafun" mean?

The word "*tzafun*" means "hidden". On the most basic level, the *Afikoman* was hidden, and then the children find it. On a deeper level, *tzafun* alludes to our freedom. While our ancestors were taken out of Egypt – redeemed from the house of bondage – the *Afikoman* reminds us that we have still not received total freedom. We are still in a type of exile, and thus the true redemption remains hidden from us. The hiding of the *Afikoman* and the children finding it, therefore, takes on a symbolic meaning. Our children, the focus of the commandment to tell the story of the Exodus, are the connection to the future redemption. Only through them will we merit fulfillment of the Exodus and our hidden freedom being revealed.

BARECH

BLESSING AFTER THE MEAL AND THIRD CUP

Pour the third cup of wine and recite Birkat HaMazon (the blessing after the meal).

A Song of Ascents.

When the Lord will return the exiles of Zion, we will be like dreamers.
Then our mouth will be filled with laughter, and our tongue with [songs of] joy.
Then the nations will say, "The Lord has done great things for them."
The Lord has done great things for us, we are joyful.
Lord, return our exiles as streams in [a dry land like] the Negev.
Those who sow in tears will reap with joyous song.
One who goes along weeping, carrying the seed bag,
will surely come [back] with [songs of] joy, carrying his sheaves.

When the Blessing after the Meal is said with a quorum of three or more males 13 years or older, the leader begins here. If ten or more, include the words in parentheses:

Gentlemen, let us bless [the Lord]!

All respond:

May the Lord be blessed from now until the end of time.

The leader responds:

May the Lord be blessed from now until the end of time.
With the permission of the masters, teachers and gentlemen,
let us bless (our God) He whose bounty we have eaten.

The others respond:

Blessed is (our God) He whose bounty we have eaten.

The leader responds:

Blessed is (our God) He whose bounty we have eaten.
Blessed is He, blessed is His name.

All who ate recite the Blessing after the Meal:

Blessed are You, Lord, our God, King of the universe,
who, in His goodness, feeds the whole world with grace, kindness and mercy.
He gives food to all flesh, for His kindness is everlasting.
And through His great, continuous goodness to us, we do not lack food,

ברך

Pour the third cup of wine and recite ברכת המזון.

שִׁיר הַמַּעֲלוֹת.
בְּשׁוּב יְהֹוָה אֶת שִׁיבַת צִיּוֹן הָיִינוּ כְּחֹלְמִים.
אָז יִמָּלֵא שְׂחוֹק פִּינוּ וּלְשׁוֹנֵנוּ רִנָּה.
אָז יֹאמְרוּ בַגּוֹיִם הִגְדִּיל יְהֹוָה לַעֲשׂוֹת עִם אֵלֶּה.
הִגְדִּיל יְהֹוָה לַעֲשׂוֹת עִמָּנוּ, הָיִינוּ שְׂמֵחִים.
שׁוּבָה יְהֹוָה אֶת שְׁבִיתֵנוּ כַּאֲפִיקִים בַּנֶּגֶב.
הַזֹּרְעִים בְּדִמְעָה בְּרִנָּה יִקְצֹרוּ.
הָלוֹךְ יֵלֵךְ וּבָכֹה נֹשֵׂא מֶשֶׁךְ הַזָּרַע,
בֹּא יָבוֹא בְרִנָּה נֹשֵׂא אֲלֻמֹּתָיו.

When ברכת המזון is said with a quorum of three or more males 13 years or older, the leader begins here. If ten or more, include the words in parentheses:

רַבּוֹתַי, נְבָרֵךְ!

All respond:

יְהִי שֵׁם יְהֹוָה מְבֹרָךְ מֵעַתָּה וְעַד עוֹלָם.

The leader responds:

יְהִי שֵׁם יְהֹוָה מְבֹרָךְ מֵעַתָּה וְעַד עוֹלָם.
בִּרְשׁוּת מָרָנָן וְרַבָּנָן וְרַבּוֹתַי,
נְבָרֵךְ (אֱלֹהֵינוּ) שֶׁאָכַלְנוּ מִשֶּׁלּוֹ.

The others respond:

בָּרוּךְ (אֱלֹהֵינוּ) שֶׁאָכַלְנוּ מִשֶּׁלּוֹ וּבְטוּבוֹ חָיִינוּ.

The leader responds:

בָּרוּךְ (אֱלֹהֵינוּ) שֶׁאָכַלְנוּ מִשֶּׁלּוֹ וּבְטוּבוֹ חָיִינוּ.
בָּרוּךְ הוּא וּבָרוּךְ שְׁמוֹ.

All who ate recite ברכת המזון:

בָּרוּךְ אַתָּה יְהֹוָה אֱלֹהֵינוּ מֶלֶךְ הָעוֹלָם,
הַזָּן אֶת הָעוֹלָם כֻּלּוֹ בְּטוּבוֹ בְּחֵן בְּחֶסֶד וּבְרַחֲמִים.
הוּא נוֹתֵן לֶחֶם לְכָל בָּשָׂר, כִּי לְעוֹלָם חַסְדּוֹ.
וּבְטוּבוֹ הַגָּדוֹל תָּמִיד לֹא חָסַר לָנוּ,

and may we never lack food,
for the sake of His great Name.
For He is Almighty God who feeds and sustains all,
and does good to all, and prepares food for all His creatures that He has created.
Blessed are You Lord, who provides food for all.

We thank You, Lord, our God, for having given as a heritage to our ancestors
a precious, good and spacious land,
and for having brought us out, Lord, our God, from the land of Egypt,
and redeemed us from the house of slavery,
and for Your covenant which You have sealed in our flesh,
and for Your Torah which You have taught us,
and for Your laws which You have made known to us,
and for the life, favor and kindness which You have graciously bestowed upon us,
and for the food we eat
with which You continuously feed and sustain us,
every day, at all times, and at every hour.

For all this, Lord, our God, we thank You and bless You.
May Your Name be blessed by the mouth of every living creature, forever and all time.
As it is written:
"And when you have eaten and are satiated, you shall bless the Lord, your God,
for the good land which He has given you."
Blessed are You, Lord, for the land and for the food.

Please have mercy, Lord, our God, upon Israel Your people, upon Jerusalem Your city,
and upon Zion the dwelling place of Your glory, upon the royal house of David Your anointed,
and upon the great and holy House that is called by Your Name.
Our God, our Father, our Shepherd, feed us, support us, nourish us and relieve us.
And relieve us, Lord, our God, speedily from all our afflictions.
And please Lord, our God, do not make us dependent upon the gifts of mortal men
or upon their loans, but only upon Your full, open, holy and generous hand,
that we may not be ashamed or disgraced forever and all time.

וְאַל יֶחְסַר לָנוּ מָזוֹן לְעוֹלָם וָעֶד,
בַּעֲבוּר שְׁמוֹ הַגָּדוֹל.
כִּי הוּא אֵל זָן וּמְפַרְנֵס לַכֹּל,
וּמֵטִיב לַכֹּל וּמֵכִין מָזוֹן לְכָל בְּרִיּוֹתָיו אֲשֶׁר בָּרָא.
בָּרוּךְ אַתָּה יְהֹוָה, הַזָּן אֶת הַכֹּל.

נוֹדֶה לְּךָ יְהֹוָה אֱלֹהֵינוּ עַל שֶׁהִנְחַלְתָּ לַאֲבוֹתֵינוּ
אֶרֶץ חֶמְדָּה טוֹבָה וּרְחָבָה,
וְעַל שֶׁהוֹצֵאתָנוּ יְהֹוָה אֱלֹהֵינוּ מֵאֶרֶץ מִצְרַיִם,
וּפְדִיתָנוּ מִבֵּית עֲבָדִים,
וְעַל בְּרִיתְךָ שֶׁחָתַמְתָּ בִּבְשָׂרֵנוּ,
וְעַל תּוֹרָתְךָ שֶׁלִּמַּדְתָּנוּ,
וְעַל חֻקֶּיךָ שֶׁהוֹדַעְתָּנוּ,
וְעַל חַיִּים, חֵן וָחֶסֶד שֶׁחוֹנַנְתָּנוּ,
וְעַל אֲכִילַת מָזוֹן
שָׁאַתָּה זָן וּמְפַרְנֵס אוֹתָנוּ תָּמִיד,
בְּכָל יוֹם וּבְכָל עֵת וּבְכָל שָׁעָה.

וְעַל הַכֹּל יְהֹוָה אֱלֹהֵינוּ אֲנַחְנוּ מוֹדִים לָךְ וּמְבָרְכִים אוֹתָךְ.
יִתְבָּרַךְ שִׁמְךָ בְּפִי כָּל חַי תָּמִיד לְעוֹלָם וָעֶד.
כַּכָּתוּב,
וְאָכַלְתָּ וְשָׂבָעְתָּ וּבֵרַכְתָּ אֶת יְהֹוָה אֱלֹהֶיךָ,
עַל הָאָרֶץ הַטֹּבָה אֲשֶׁר נָתַן לָךְ.
בָּרוּךְ אַתָּה יְהֹוָה, עַל הָאָרֶץ וְעַל הַמָּזוֹן.

רַחֵם נָא יְהֹוָה אֱלֹהֵינוּ עַל יִשְׂרָאֵל עַמֶּךָ, וְעַל יְרוּשָׁלַיִם עִירֶךָ,
וְעַל צִיּוֹן מִשְׁכַּן כְּבוֹדֶךָ, וְעַל מַלְכוּת בֵּית דָּוִד מְשִׁיחֶךָ,
וְעַל הַבַּיִת הַגָּדוֹל וְהַקָּדוֹשׁ שֶׁנִּקְרָא שִׁמְךָ עָלָיו.
אֱלֹהֵינוּ, אָבִינוּ, רְעֵנוּ זוּנֵנוּ פַּרְנְסֵנוּ וְכַלְכְּלֵנוּ וְהַרְוִיחֵנוּ.
וְהַרְוַח לָנוּ יְהֹוָה אֱלֹהֵינוּ מְהֵרָה מִכָּל צָרוֹתֵינוּ.
וְנָא אַל תַּצְרִיכֵנוּ יְהֹוָה אֱלֹהֵינוּ לֹא לִידֵי מַתְּנַת בָּשָׂר וָדָם
וְלֹא לִידֵי הַלְוָאָתָם כִּי אִם לְיָדְךָ הַמְּלֵאָה, הַפְּתוּחָה, הַקְּדוֹשָׁה וְהָרְחָבָה,
שֶׁלֹּא נֵבוֹשׁ וְלֹא נִכָּלֵם לְעוֹלָם וָעֶד.

On Shabbat add:

Favor and strengthen us, Lord, our God, through Your commandments,
and through the commandment of the seventh day, this great and holy Shabbat.
For this day is great and holy before You, to cease work thereon,
and to rest thereon with love, in accordance with the commandment of Your will.
And may it be Your will, to bestow upon us tranquility, Lord, our God,
that there shall be no trouble, sadness or grief on the day of our rest.
And may You show us Lord, our God, the consolation of Zion, Your city,
and the rebuilding of Jerusalem, Your holy city,
for You are the Master of salvations and the Master of consolations.

Our God and God of our forefathers,
may there ascend and come, and reach and be seen,
and accepted, and heard, and recalled, and remembered,
the remembrance of us and the recollection of us, and the remembrance of our forefathers,
and the remembrance of Mashiach, the son of David, Your servant,
the remembrance of Jerusalem Your holy city,
and the remembrance of all Your people, the House of Israel, before You,
for deliverance, well-being, grace, kindness, mercy, good life and peace
on this day of the Festival of Matzot.
Remember us, Lord, our God, on this [day] for good,
and recollect us on this [day] for a blessing,
and deliver us on this [day] for good life.
In accord with the promise of deliverance and compassion,
spare us and be gracious to us, and have compassion upon us and deliver us,
for our eyes are turned to You,
because You are the Almighty King, gracious and merciful.

And rebuild Jerusalem,
the holy city, speedily in our days.
Blessed are You, Lord, who in His mercy rebuilds Jerusalem. Amen.

Blessed are You, Lord, our God, King of the universe,
the Almighty God, our Father, our King, our Might, our Creator, our Redeemer, our Creator,

On שבת add:

רְצֵה וְהַחֲלִיצֵנוּ יְהֹוָה אֱלֹהֵינוּ בְּמִצְוֹתֶיךָ,
וּבְמִצְוַת יוֹם הַשְּׁבִיעִי הַשַּׁבָּת הַגָּדוֹל וְהַקָּדוֹשׁ הַזֶּה.
כִּי יוֹם זֶה גָּדוֹל וְקָדוֹשׁ הוּא לְפָנֶיךָ לִשְׁבָּת בּוֹ,
וְלָנוּחַ בּוֹ בְּאַהֲבָה כְּמִצְוַת רְצוֹנֶךָ.
וּבִרְצוֹנְךָ הָנִיחַ לָנוּ יְהֹוָה אֱלֹהֵינוּ,
שֶׁלֹּא תְהֵא צָרָה וְיָגוֹן וַאֲנָחָה בְּיוֹם מְנוּחָתֵנוּ.
וְהַרְאֵנוּ יְהֹוָה אֱלֹהֵינוּ בְּנֶחָמַת צִיּוֹן עִירֶךָ,
וּבְבִנְיַן יְרוּשָׁלַיִם עִיר קָדְשֶׁךָ,
כִּי אַתָּה הוּא בַּעַל הַיְשׁוּעוֹת וּבַעַל הַנֶּחָמוֹת.

אֱלֹהֵינוּ וֵאלֹהֵי אֲבוֹתֵינוּ,
יַעֲלֶה וְיָבֹא וְיַגִּיעַ וְיֵרָאֶה,
וְיֵרָצֶה וְיִשָּׁמַע וְיִפָּקֵד וְיִזָּכֵר
זִכְרוֹנֵנוּ, וּפִקְדוֹנֵנוּ וְזִכְרוֹן אֲבוֹתֵינוּ,
וְזִכְרוֹן מָשִׁיחַ בֶּן דָּוִד עַבְדֶּךָ,
וְזִכְרוֹן יְרוּשָׁלַיִם עִיר קָדְשֶׁךָ,
וְזִכְרוֹן כָּל עַמְּךָ בֵּית יִשְׂרָאֵל לְפָנֶיךָ,
לִפְלֵיטָה, לְטוֹבָה, לְחֵן וּלְחֶסֶד וּלְרַחֲמִים, לְחַיִּים וּלְשָׁלוֹם
בְּיוֹם חַג הַמַּצּוֹת הַזֶּה.
זָכְרֵנוּ יְהֹוָה אֱלֹהֵינוּ בּוֹ לְטוֹבָה,
וּפָקְדֵנוּ בוֹ לִבְרָכָה,
וְהוֹשִׁיעֵנוּ בוֹ לְחַיִּים טוֹבִים.
וּבִדְבַר יְשׁוּעָה וְרַחֲמִים,
חוּס וְחָנֵּנוּ וְרַחֵם עָלֵינוּ וְהוֹשִׁיעֵנוּ,
כִּי אֵלֶיךָ עֵינֵינוּ,
כִּי אֵל מֶלֶךְ חַנּוּן וְרַחוּם אָתָּה.

וּבְנֵה יְרוּשָׁלַיִם

עִיר הַקֹּדֶשׁ בִּמְהֵרָה בְיָמֵינוּ.
בָּרוּךְ אַתָּה יְהֹוָה, בּוֹנֵה בְרַחֲמָיו יְרוּשָׁלָיִם. אָמֵן.

בָּרוּךְ אַתָּה יְהֹוָה אֱלֹהֵינוּ מֶלֶךְ הָעוֹלָם,
הָאֵל אָבִינוּ מַלְכֵּנוּ אַדִּירֵנוּ בּוֹרְאֵנוּ גּוֹאֲלֵנוּ יוֹצְרֵנוּ,

our Holy One, the Holy One of Jacob, our Shepherd, the Shepherd of Israel,
the King who is good and does good to all, each and every day.
He has done good for us, He does good for us, and He will do good for us.
He has bestowed, He bestows, and He will bestow upon us forever,
grace, kindness and mercy, relief, salvation and success,
blessing and salvation, consolation, sustenance and nourishment,
and compassion, life, peace and all goodness,
and may He never cause us to lack any good.

May the Merciful One reign over us forever and all time.

May the Merciful One be blessed in heaven and on earth.

May the Merciful One be praised from generation to generation,
and be glorified in us forever and all eternity,
and honored among us forever and for all time.

May the Merciful One sustain us with honor.

May the Merciful One break the yoke of exile from our neck,
and may He lead us upright to our land.

May the Merciful One send abundant blessings to this house,
and upon this table upon which we have eaten.

May the Merciful One send us Elijah the Prophet, may he be remembered for good,
and may he bring us good tidings, salvation and consolation.

קְדוֹשֵׁנוּ קְדוֹשׁ יַעֲקֹב, רוֹעֵנוּ רוֹעֵה יִשְׂרָאֵל,
הַמֶּלֶךְ הַטּוֹב וְהַמֵּטִיב לַכֹּל, שֶׁבְּכָל יוֹם וָיוֹם.
הוּא הֵטִיב, הוּא מֵטִיב, הוּא יֵטִיב לָנוּ.
הוּא גְמָלָנוּ, הוּא גוֹמְלֵנוּ, הוּא יִגְמְלֵנוּ לָעַד,
לְחֵן וּלְחֶסֶד וּלְרַחֲמִים וּלְרֶוַח, הַצָּלָה וְהַצְלָחָה,
בְּרָכָה וִישׁוּעָה, נֶחָמָה, פַּרְנָסָה וְכַלְכָּלָה,
וְרַחֲמִים וְחַיִּים וְשָׁלוֹם וְכָל טוֹב,
וּמִכָּל טוּב לְעוֹלָם אַל יְחַסְּרֵנוּ.

הָרַחֲמָן הוּא יִמְלֹךְ עָלֵינוּ לְעוֹלָם וָעֶד.

הָרַחֲמָן הוּא יִתְבָּרַךְ בַּשָּׁמַיִם וּבָאָרֶץ.

הָרַחֲמָן הוּא יִשְׁתַּבַּח לְדוֹר דּוֹרִים,
וְיִתְפָּאַר בָּנוּ לָעַד וּלְנֵצַח נְצָחִים,
וְיִתְהַדַּר בָּנוּ לָעַד וּלְעוֹלְמֵי עוֹלָמִים.

הָרַחֲמָן הוּא יְפַרְנְסֵנוּ בְּכָבוֹד.

הָרַחֲמָן הוּא יִשְׁבֹּר עֻלֵּנוּ מֵעַל צַוָּארֵנוּ,
וְהוּא יוֹלִיכֵנוּ קוֹמְמִיּוּת לְאַרְצֵנוּ.

הָרַחֲמָן הוּא יִשְׁלַח לָנוּ בְּרָכָה מְרֻבָּה בַּבַּיִת הַזֶּה,
וְעַל שֻׁלְחָן זֶה שֶׁאָכַלְנוּ עָלָיו.

הָרַחֲמָן הוּא יִשְׁלַח לָנוּ אֶת אֵלִיָּהוּ הַנָּבִיא זָכוּר לַטּוֹב,
וִיבַשֶּׂר לָנוּ בְּשׂוֹרוֹת טוֹבוֹת, יְשׁוּעוֹת וְנֶחָמוֹת.

May the Merciful One bless:

One eating at his or her own table says (include the words that apply):

me, (and my wife/husband, and my children)
and all that is mine,

A guest at another's table says (including the words that apply):

the master of this house and the mistress of this house,
and their household (and their children)
and all that is theirs,

A child at a parent's table says (including the words that apply):

my father, my teacher (master of this house),
and my mother, my teacher (mistress of this house),
them, their household, their children, and all that is theirs,

All guests add:

us, and all that is ours,

All continue:

just as our forefathers, Abraham, Isaac and Jacob were blessed
in all, from all, with all, so may He bless all of us together
with a complete blessing. And let us say, Amen.

From On High, may there be invoked upon them and upon us
such merit which will bring a safeguard of peace.
May we receive blessing from the Lord and just kindness from the God of our salvation,
and may we find grace and good understanding in the eyes of God and man.

On Shabbat add:

May the Merciful One cause us to inherit that day
which will be Shabbat in entirety and rest for life everlasting.

May the Merciful One cause us to inherit that day that is all good.

May the Merciful One grant us the privilege of reaching the days of the Messiah
and the life of the World to Come.

הָרַחֲמָן הוּא יְבָרֵךְ:

One eating at his or her own table says (include the words that apply):

אוֹתִי (וְאֶת אִשְׁתִּי/אִישִׁי וְאֶת זַרְעִי)
וְאֶת כָּל אֲשֶׁר לִי,

A guest at another's table says (including the words that apply):

אֶת בַּעַל הַבַּיִת הַזֶּה וְאֶת בַּעֲלַת הַבַּיִת הַזֶּה,
וְאֶת בֵּיתָם (וְאֶת זַרְעָם)
וְאֶת כָּל אֲשֶׁר לָהֶם,

A child at a parent's table says (including the words that apply):

אֶת אָבִי מוֹרִי (בַּעַל הַבַּיִת הַזֶּה)
וְאֶת אִמִּי מוֹרָתִי (בַּעֲלַת הַבַּיִת הַזֶּה)
אוֹתָם וְאֶת בֵּיתָם וְאֶת זַרְעָם וְאֶת כָּל אֲשֶׁר לָהֶם,

All guests add:

אוֹתָנוּ וְאֶת כָּל אֲשֶׁר לָנוּ,

All continue:

כְּמוֹ שֶׁנִּתְבָּרְכוּ אֲבוֹתֵינוּ אַבְרָהָם יִצְחָק וְיַעֲקֹב
בַּכֹּל, מִכֹּל, כֹּל, כֵּן יְבָרֵךְ אוֹתָנוּ כֻּלָּנוּ יַחַד
בִּבְרָכָה שְׁלֵמָה. וְנֹאמַר אָמֵן.

בַּמָּרוֹם יְלַמְּדוּ עֲלֵיהֶם וְעָלֵינוּ
זְכוּת שֶׁתְּהֵא לְמִשְׁמֶרֶת שָׁלוֹם.
וְנִשָּׂא בְרָכָה מֵאֵת יְהֹוָה וּצְדָקָה מֵאֱלֹהֵי יִשְׁעֵנוּ,
וְנִמְצָא חֵן וְשֵׂכֶל טוֹב בְּעֵינֵי אֱלֹהִים וְאָדָם.

On שבת add:

הָרַחֲמָן הוּא יַנְחִילֵנוּ יוֹם שֶׁכֻּלּוֹ
שַׁבָּת וּמְנוּחָה לְחַיֵּי הָעוֹלָמִים.

הָרַחֲמָן הוּא יַנְחִילֵנוּ יוֹם שֶׁכֻּלּוֹ טוֹב.

הָרַחֲמָן הוּא יְזַכֵּנוּ לִימוֹת הַמָּשִׁיחַ
וּלְחַיֵּי הָעוֹלָם הַבָּא.

He is a tower of salvation to His king, and bestows kindness upon His anointed,
to David, and to his descendants until the end of time.
He who makes peace in His heights,
may He make peace for us and for all Israel.
And let us say, Amen!

Fear the Lord, [you], His holy ones, for those who fear Him suffer no want.
Young lions are in need and go hungry,
but those who seek the Lord shall not lack any good.
Give thanks to the Lord for He is good, for His kindness is everlasting.
[You] open Your hand and satisfy the desire of every living thing.
Blessed is the person who trusts in the Lord, and the Lord shall be his security.
I was young, and now I am old,
yet I have never seen a righteous man forsaken or his children begging for bread.
The Lord will give His people strength.
The Lord will bless His people with peace.

Recite the blessing for the wine, and drink in a reclining position.

Blessed are You, Lord, our God, King of the universe,
who creates the fruit of the vine.

מִגְדּוֹל יְשׁוּעוֹת מַלְכּוֹ וְעֹשֶׂה חֶסֶד לִמְשִׁיחוֹ,
לְדָוִד וּלְזַרְעוֹ עַד עוֹלָם.
עֹשֶׂה שָׁלוֹם בִּמְרוֹמָיו,
הוּא יַעֲשֶׂה שָׁלוֹם עָלֵינוּ וְעַל כָּל יִשְׂרָאֵל.
וְאִמְרוּ אָמֵן!

יְראוּ אֶת יְהֹוָה קְדֹשָׁיו כִּי אֵין מַחְסוֹר לִירֵאָיו.
כְּפִירִים רָשׁוּ וְרָעֵבוּ,
וְדֹרְשֵׁי יְהֹוָה לֹא יַחְסְרוּ כָל טוֹב.
הוֹדוּ לַיהֹוָה כִּי טוֹב, כִּי לְעוֹלָם חַסְדּוֹ.
פּוֹתֵחַ אֶת יָדֶךָ, וּמַשְׂבִּיעַ לְכָל חַי רָצוֹן.
בָּרוּךְ הַגֶּבֶר אֲשֶׁר יִבְטַח בַּיהֹוָה וְהָיָה יְהֹוָה מִבְטַחוֹ.
נַעַר הָיִיתִי גַּם זָקַנְתִּי,
וְלֹא רָאִיתִי צַדִּיק נֶעֱזָב, וְזַרְעוֹ מְבַקֶּשׁ לָחֶם.
יְהֹוָה עֹז לְעַמּוֹ יִתֵּן.
יְהֹוָה יְבָרֵךְ אֶת עַמּוֹ בַשָּׁלוֹם.

Recite the ברכה *for the wine, and drink in a reclining position.*

בָּרוּךְ אַתָּה יְהֹוָה אֱלֹהֵינוּ מֶלֶךְ הָעוֹלָם,
בּוֹרֵא פְּרִי הַגָּפֶן.

Welcoming Elijah the Prophet

The fourth cup is poured. Open the door to symbolically welcome Elijah.

Say the following:

Pour out Your wrath

upon the nations that do not acknowledge You,
and upon the kingdoms that do not call upon Your Name.
For they have devoured Jacob and laid waste his habitation.
Pour out Your indignation upon them,
and let the fierceness of Your anger overtake them.
Pursue them with anger,
and destroy them from beneath the heavens of the Lord.

Why do we pour a cup of wine for Elijah?

The scriptural basis for the four cups of wine is the passage in the book of Exodus that states "I will take you out", "I will save you", "I will redeem you", and "I will take you as a nation" which are God's promises of redemption. However, those promises are followed by a fifth promise, "And I will bring you to the land which I promised Abraham, Isaac, and Jacob, and I will give it to you as an inheritance." Although the first four promises were fulfilled, the final, fifth promise has yet to be fully realized. In recognition of this, just as the four fulfilled promises are represented by four cups of wine, the final, unfulfilled promise is represented by a fifth cup, which remains undrunk, awaiting the arrival of Elijah the Prophet, whose presence will usher in the Messianic age and the ultimate fulfillment of the fifth promise.

What alternative is there to this passage, "Pour out Your wrath"?

The following passage is attributed to a 16th century *Haggadah* manuscript and has been incorporated in many modern *Haggadot*:

שְׁפֹךְ אַהֲבָתְךָ עַל הַגּוֹיִים אֲשֶׁר יְדָעוּךָ,	Pour out Your love upon the nations who have known You,
וְעַל מַמְלָכוֹת אֲשֶׁר בְּשִׁמְךָ קוֹרְאִים,	and upon the kingdoms who call upon your Name.
בִּגְלַל חֲסָדִים שֶׁהֵם עוֹשִׂים עִם יַעֲקֹב,	For they show loving-kindness to the seed of Jacob,
וּמְגִנִּים עַל עַמְּךָ יִשְׂרָאֵל	and they defend Your people Israel
מִפְּנֵי אוֹכְלֵיהֶם,	from those who would devour them alive.
יִזְכּוּ לִרְאוֹת בְּסֻכַּת בְּחִירֶיךָ,	May they live to see the sukkah of peace over Your chosen,
וְלִשְׂמֹחַ בְּשִׂמְחַת גּוֹיֶיךָ,	and to participate in the joy of Your nations.

אליהו הנביא

The fourth cup is poured. Open the door to symbolically welcome אליהו.

Say the following:

שְׁפֹךְ חֲמָתְךָ

אֶל הַגּוֹיִם אֲשֶׁר לֹא יְדָעוּךָ,
וְעַל מַמְלָכוֹת אֲשֶׁר בְּשִׁמְךָ לֹא קָרָאוּ.
כִּי אָכַל אֶת יַעֲקֹב וְאֶת נָוֵהוּ הֵשַׁמּוּ.
שְׁפָךְ עֲלֵיהֶם זַעְמֶךָ,
וַחֲרוֹן אַפְּךָ יַשִּׂיגֵם.
תִּרְדֹּף בְּאַף,
וְתַשְׁמִידֵם מִתַּחַת שְׁמֵי יְהֹוָה.

Q&A

What song is traditionally sung at this point?

.Eliyahu haNavi, Eliyahu haTishbi, Eliyahu haGiladi, bimheira yavo, eilienu im mashi'ach ben David

אֵלִיָּהוּ הַנָּבִיא אֵלִיָּהוּ הַתִּשְׁבִּי אֵלִיָּהוּ הַגִּלְעָדִי בִּמְהֵרָה יָבוֹא אֵלֵינוּ עִם מָשִׁיחַ בֶּן דָּוִד

Why is this passage, "Pour out Your wrath", included in the *Haggadah*?

This passage is a late edition to the *Haggadah*. It was first included during the First Crusade, when entire Jewish communities were massacred by Crusaders on their way to the Holy Land, setting off a long history of persecution that included a litany of further massacres, inquisitions, pogroms, blood libels, and ultimately the Holocaust. Despite the many catastrophes that befell the Jewish people, this passage is the only one that recalls tragic events outside of the Exodus. While it may seem on its face to be a demand for vengeance, rather it is a cry for divine justice. Judaism is a religion of justice. Just as God demands that Jews pursue justice, we too demand that God deliver justice, just as both Abraham and the Psalmist demanded that God deliver justice.

Why do we open the door for Elijah the Prophet at this point?

The call for justice in the form of God pouring out His wrath is a hopeful plea for the days of the Messiah. At that time, we expect that justice will be served. In that hope, we open the door to Elijah the Prophet, whose appearance will herald the coming of the Messiah and the peaceful world that his presence will inaugurate. Opening the door is also a statement that Elijah cannot come, and the Messianic age cannot begin, without us doing our part. We must open the door for him, as if symbolically to demonstrate our actions and our faith that will make his arrival, and the Messianic age, possible.

HALLEL
PSALMS OF PRAISE AND FOURTH CUP

Not to us, Lord, not to us, but to Your Name give glory,
for Your kindness and for Your truth.
Why should the nations say, "Where, now, is their God?"
Our God is in heaven, whatever He desires, He does.
Their idols are of silver and gold, the product of human hands:
They have a mouth, but cannot speak; they have eyes, but cannot see.
They have ears, but cannot hear; they have a nose, but cannot smell.
[They have] their hands, but cannot feel; [they have] their feet, but cannot walk.
They can make no sound with their throat.
Those who make them will become like them, everyone who trusts in them.
Israel, trust in the Lord! He is their help and their shield.
House of Aaron, trust in the Lord! He is their help and their shield.
Those who fear the Lord, trust in the Lord! He is their help and their shield.

---

are those alluding to the coming of the times of the Messiah, such as "Praise the Lord, all nations! Extol Him, all peoples!" Thus, the portion of the *Haggadah* that precedes the meal focuses on the past, while after the meal the focus is on the future. Looking forward to the future is appropriate at this point in the *Haggadah* because we have just welcomed Elijah the Prophet, who will usher in the Messianic era.

For a transliteration of the Hebrew text, please turn to page 172.

The Lord remembers us and will bless [us].
He will bless the House of Israel; He will bless the House of Aaron.
He will bless those who fear the Lord, the small with the great.
May the Lord increase [blessing] upon you, upon you and upon your children.
May you be blessed unto the Lord, the Maker of heaven and earth.
The heavens are the heavens of the Lord, but the earth He gave to Mankind.
The dead do not praise the Lord, nor do those that go down into silence [of the grave].
But we will bless the Lord, from now until the end of time.
Halleluyah!

הלל

לֹא לָנוּ יְהֹוָה לֹא לָנוּ, כִּי לְשִׁמְךָ תֵּן כָּבוֹד,
עַל חַסְדְּךָ עַל אֲמִתֶּךָ.
לָמָּה יֹאמְרוּ הַגּוֹיִם אַיֵּה נָא אֱלֹהֵיהֶם?
וֵאלֹהֵינוּ בַשָּׁמָיִם כֹּל אֲשֶׁר חָפֵץ עָשָׂה.
עֲצַבֵּיהֶם כֶּסֶף וְזָהָב מַעֲשֵׂה יְדֵי אָדָם:
פֶּה לָהֶם וְלֹא יְדַבֵּרוּ, עֵינַיִם לָהֶם וְלֹא יִרְאוּ.
אָזְנַיִם לָהֶם וְלֹא יִשְׁמָעוּ, אַף לָהֶם וְלֹא יְרִיחוּן.
יְדֵיהֶם וְלֹא יְמִישׁוּן, רַגְלֵיהֶם וְלֹא יְהַלֵּכוּ.
לֹא יֶהְגּוּ בִּגְרוֹנָם.
כְּמוֹהֶם יִהְיוּ עֹשֵׂיהֶם, כֹּל אֲשֶׁר בֹּטֵחַ בָּהֶם.
יִשְׂרָאֵל בְּטַח בַּיהֹוָה. עֶזְרָם וּמָגִנָּם הוּא.
בֵּית אַהֲרֹן בִּטְחוּ בַיהֹוָה. עֶזְרָם וּמָגִנָּם הוּא.
יִרְאֵי יְהֹוָה בִּטְחוּ בַיהֹוָה. עֶזְרָם וּמָגִנָּם הוּא.

Q&A

Why is the *Hallel* split between the sections Magid and Hallel?

Isaac ben Yehuda Abarbanel, a Portuguese rabbi in the 15th century, explained why the *Hallel* is split in two in the *Haggadah*. The first part of the *Hallel* commemorates the miracles that have already occurred. It includes praises of God for having "brought us out from slavery to freedom". The second half of the *Hallel* includes praises of God for the miracles that are yet to come. Among those praises

For a transliteration of the following text, please turn to page 172.

יְהֹוָה זְכָרָנוּ יְבָרֵךְ.
יְבָרֵךְ אֶת בֵּית יִשְׂרָאֵל, יְבָרֵךְ אֶת בֵּית אַהֲרֹן.
יְבָרֵךְ יִרְאֵי יְהֹוָה, הַקְּטַנִּים עִם הַגְּדֹלִים.
יֹסֵף יְהֹוָה עֲלֵיכֶם, עֲלֵיכֶם וְעַל בְּנֵיכֶם.
בְּרוּכִים אַתֶּם לַיהֹוָה, עֹשֵׂה שָׁמַיִם וָאָרֶץ.
הַשָּׁמַיִם שָׁמַיִם לַיהֹוָה, וְהָאָרֶץ נָתַן לִבְנֵי אָדָם.
לֹא הַמֵּתִים יְהַלְלוּ יָהּ, וְלֹא כָּל יֹרְדֵי דוּמָה.
וַאֲנַחְנוּ נְבָרֵךְ יָהּ, מֵעַתָּה וְעַד עוֹלָם.
הַלְלוּיָהּ!

I love the Lord, because He hears my voice, my pleas.
For He turns His ear to me, all my days I will call [upon Him].
The pangs of death encompassed me, and the agonies of the grave came upon me,
trouble and sorrow I encounter.
And I call upon the Name of the Lord: Please, Lord, deliver my soul!
Gracious is the Lord, and just, and our God is compassionate.
The Lord watches over the simpletons; I was brought low and He saved me.
Return, my soul, to your rest, for the Lord has dealt kindly with you.
For You have delivered my soul from death, my eyes from tears, my foot from stumbling.
I will walk before the Lord in the lands of the living.
I had faith even when I said, "I am greatly afflicted".
[Even when] I said in my haste, "All men are deceitful."

For a transliteration of the Hebrew text, please turn to page 172.

What can I repay the Lord for all His kindness to me?
I will raise the cup of salvation and call upon the Name of the Lord.
I will fulfill my vows to the Lord in the presence of all His people.
Grievous in the eyes of the Lord is the death of His pious ones.
I thank you, Lord, for I am Your servant; I am Your servant, the son of Your handmaid.
You have loosened my bonds.
To You I will bring an offering of thanksgiving,
and I will call upon the Name of the Lord.
I will fulfill my vows to the Lord in the presence of all His people,
in the courtyards of the House of the Lord, in the midst of Jerusalem.
Halleluyah!

Praise the Lord, all nations! Extol Him, all peoples!
For His kindness to us was mighty, and the truth of the Lord is everlasting.
Halleluyah!

Give thanks to the Lord, for He is good, for His kindness is everlasting!
Let Israel say, for His kindness is everlasting!
Let the House of Aaron say, for His kindness is everlasting!
Let those who fear the Lord say, for His kindness is everlasting!

אָהַבְתִּי כִּי יִשְׁמַע יְהֹוָה אֶת קוֹלִי תַּחֲנוּנָי.
כִּי הִטָּה אָזְנוֹ לִי וּבְיָמַי אֶקְרָא.
אֲפָפוּנִי חֶבְלֵי מָוֶת וּמְצָרֵי שְׁאוֹל מְצָאוּנִי,
צָרָה וְיָגוֹן אֶמְצָא.
וּבְשֵׁם יְהֹוָה אֶקְרָא אָנָּא יְהֹוָה מַלְּטָה נַפְשִׁי.
חַנּוּן יְהֹוָה וְצַדִּיק וֵאלֹהֵינוּ מְרַחֵם.
שֹׁמֵר פְּתָאִים יְהֹוָה דַּלּוֹתִי וְלִי יְהוֹשִׁיעַ.
שׁוּבִי נַפְשִׁי לִמְנוּחָיְכִי כִּי יְהֹוָה גָּמַל עָלָיְכִי.
כִּי חִלַּצְתָּ נַפְשִׁי מִמָּוֶת אֶת עֵינִי מִן דִּמְעָה אֶת רַגְלִי מִדֶּחִי.
אֶתְהַלֵּךְ לִפְנֵי יְהֹוָה בְּאַרְצוֹת הַחַיִּים.
הֶאֱמַנְתִּי כִּי אֲדַבֵּר אֲנִי עָנִיתִי מְאֹד.
אֲנִי אָמַרְתִּי בְחָפְזִי כָּל הָאָדָם כֹּזֵב.

For a transliteration of the following text, please turn to page 172.

מָה אָשִׁיב לַיהֹוָה כָּל תַּגְמוּלוֹהִי עָלָי.
כּוֹס יְשׁוּעוֹת אֶשָּׂא וּבְשֵׁם יְהֹוָה אֶקְרָא.
נְדָרַי לַיהֹוָה אֲשַׁלֵּם נֶגְדָה נָּא לְכָל עַמּוֹ.
יָקָר בְּעֵינֵי יְהֹוָה הַמָּוְתָה לַחֲסִידָיו.
אָנָּה יְהֹוָה כִּי אֲנִי עַבְדֶּךָ, אֲנִי עַבְדְּךָ בֶּן אֲמָתֶךָ.
פִּתַּחְתָּ לְמוֹסֵרָי.
לְךָ אֶזְבַּח זֶבַח תּוֹדָה,
וּבְשֵׁם יְהֹוָה אֶקְרָא.
לַיהֹוָה אֲשַׁלֵּם נֶגְדָה נָּא לְכָל עַמּוֹ,
בְּחַצְרוֹת בֵּית יְהֹוָה בְּתוֹכֵכִי יְרוּשָׁלָיִם.
הַלְלוּיָהּ!

הַלְלוּ אֶת יְהֹוָה כָּל גּוֹיִם, שַׁבְּחוּהוּ כָּל הָאֻמִּים.
כִּי גָבַר עָלֵינוּ חַסְדּוֹ וֶאֱמֶת יְהֹוָה לְעוֹלָם.
הַלְלוּיָהּ!

הוֹדוּ לַיהֹוָה כִּי טוֹב, כִּי לְעוֹלָם חַסְדּוֹ.
יֹאמַר נָא יִשְׂרָאֵל, כִּי לְעוֹלָם חַסְדּוֹ.
יֹאמְרוּ נָא בֵית אַהֲרֹן, כִּי לְעוֹלָם חַסְדּוֹ.
יֹאמְרוּ נָא יִרְאֵי יְהֹוָה, כִּי לְעוֹלָם חַסְדּוֹ.

Out of distress I called to the Lord, the Lord answered me with abounding relief.
The Lord is with me, I will not fear. What can man do to me?
The Lord is with me, through my helpers, and I will see [the downfall of] my enemies.
It is better to rely on the Lord, than to trust in man.
It is better to rely on the Lord, than to trust in nobles.
All nations surround me, but I cut them down in the Name of the Lord.
They surrounded me, also encompassed me,
[yet] I cut them down in the Name of the Lord.
They surrounded me like bees, [yet] they are extinguished like fiery thorns.
I cut them down in the Name of the Lord.
You [my foes] pushed and pushed me [again] to fall, but the Lord helped me.
The Lord is my strength and song, and this has been my salvation.
The sound of [songs of] joy and salvation is in the tents of the righteous:
"The right hand of the Lord performs [deeds of] valor, the right hand of the Lord is exalted,
the right hand of the Lord performs [deeds of] valor!"
I shall not die, but I shall live and relate the deeds of the Lord.
The Lord has chastised me, but He did not give me over to death.
Open for me the gates of righteousness, I will enter them and give thanks to the Lord.
This is the gate of the Lord, the righteous will enter it.

I thank You for You have answered me, and You have been my salvation.
    I thank You for You have answered me, and You have been my salvation.
The stone scorned by the builders has become the cornerstone.
    The stone scorned by the builders has become the cornerstone.
This was indeed from the Lord, it is wondrous in our eyes.
    This was indeed from the Lord, it is wondrous in our eyes.
This day the Lord has made, let us be glad and rejoice on it.
    This day the Lord has made, let us be glad and rejoice on it.

Please, Lord, help us!
    Please, Lord, help us!
Please, Lord, grant us success!
    Please, Lord, grant us success!

מִן הַמֵּצַר קָרָאתִי יָּהּ, עָנָנִי בַמֶּרְחַב יָהּ.
יְהֹוָה לִי לֹא אִירָא. מַה יַּעֲשֶׂה לִי אָדָם?
יְהֹוָה לִי בְּעֹזְרָי, וַאֲנִי אֶרְאֶה בְשֹׂנְאָי.
טוֹב לַחֲסוֹת בַּיהֹוָה, מִבְּטֹחַ בָּאָדָם.
טוֹב לַחֲסוֹת בַּיהֹוָה, מִבְּטֹחַ בִּנְדִיבִים.
כָּל גּוֹיִם סְבָבוּנִי, בְּשֵׁם יְהֹוָה כִּי אֲמִילַם.
סַבּוּנִי גַם סְבָבוּנִי,
בְּשֵׁם יְהֹוָה כִּי אֲמִילַם.
סַבּוּנִי כִדְבֹרִים, דֹּעֲכוּ כְּאֵשׁ קוֹצִים.
בְּשֵׁם יְהֹוָה כִּי אֲמִילַם.
דָּחֹה דְחִיתַנִי לִנְפֹּל, וַיהֹוָה עֲזָרָנִי.
עָזִּי וְזִמְרָת יָהּ, וַיְהִי לִי לִישׁוּעָה.
קוֹל רִנָּה וִישׁוּעָה בְּאָהֳלֵי צַדִּיקִים,
יְמִין יְהֹוָה עֹשָׂה חָיִל, יְמִין יְהֹוָה רוֹמֵמָה,
יְמִין יְהֹוָה עֹשָׂה חָיִל.
לֹא אָמוּת, כִּי אֶחְיֶה וַאֲסַפֵּר מַעֲשֵׂי יָהּ.
יַסֹּר יִסְּרַנִּי יָּהּ, וְלַמָּוֶת לֹא נְתָנָנִי.
פִּתְחוּ לִי שַׁעֲרֵי צֶדֶק, אָבֹא בָם אוֹדֶה יָהּ.
זֶה הַשַּׁעַר לַיהֹוָה, צַדִּיקִים יָבֹאוּ בוֹ.

אוֹדְךָ כִּי עֲנִיתָנִי, וַתְּהִי לִי לִישׁוּעָה.
אוֹדְךָ כִּי עֲנִיתָנִי, וַתְּהִי לִי לִישׁוּעָה.
אֶבֶן מָאֲסוּ הַבּוֹנִים הָיְתָה לְרֹאשׁ פִּנָּה.
אֶבֶן מָאֲסוּ הַבּוֹנִים הָיְתָה לְרֹאשׁ פִּנָּה.
מֵאֵת יְהֹוָה הָיְתָה זֹּאת, הִיא נִפְלָאת בְּעֵינֵינוּ.
מֵאֵת יְהֹוָה הָיְתָה זֹּאת, הִיא נִפְלָאת בְּעֵינֵינוּ.
זֶה הַיּוֹם עָשָׂה יְהֹוָה, נָגִילָה וְנִשְׂמְחָה בוֹ.
זֶה הַיּוֹם עָשָׂה יְהֹוָה, נָגִילָה וְנִשְׂמְחָה בוֹ.

אָנָּא יְהֹוָה הוֹשִׁיעָה נָּא!
אָנָּא יְהֹוָה הוֹשִׁיעָה נָּא!
אָנָּא יְהֹוָה הַצְלִיחָה נָא!
אָנָּא יְהֹוָה הַצְלִיחָה נָא!

Blessed is the one who comes in the Name of the Lord,
we bless you from the House of the Lord.
Blessed is the one who comes in the Name of the Lord,
we bless you from the House of the Lord.

The Almighty is the Lord, He gave us light,
bind the festival-offering until [you bring it to] the horns of the altar.
The Almighty is the Lord, He gave us light,
bind the festival-offering until [you bring it to] the horns of the altar.

For a transliteration of the Hebrew text, please turn to page 174.

You are my God and I will thank You,
my God, I will exalt You.
You are my God and I will thank You,
my God, I will exalt You.

Thank the Lord, for He is good,
for His kindness is everlasting.
Thank the Lord, for He is good,
for His kindness is everlasting.

All Your works, Lord, our God, will praise You,
Your pious ones, the righteous who do Your will,
and all Your people, the House of Israel, with [songs of] joy will thank and bless,
and laud and glorify and exalt and adore,
and sanctify and proclaim the sovereignty of Your Name, our King.
For it is good to thank You, and befitting to sing to Your Name,
for from the beginning until the end of time, You are Almighty God.

Give thanks to the Lord, for He is good, for His kindness is everlasting.
Give thanks to the God of the gods [celestial powers], for His kindness is everlasting.
Give thanks to the Lord of lords, for His kindness is everlasting.
Who alone does great wonders, for His kindness is everlasting.
Who made the heavens with understanding, for His kindness is everlasting.
Who spread out the earth above the waters, for His kindness is everlasting.

בָּרוּךְ הַבָּא בְּשֵׁם יְהֹוָה,
בֵּרַכְנוּכֶם מִבֵּית יְהֹוָה.
בָּרוּךְ הַבָּא בְּשֵׁם יְהֹוָה,
בֵּרַכְנוּכֶם מִבֵּית יְהֹוָה.

אֵל יְהֹוָה וַיָּאֶר לָנוּ,
אִסְרוּ חַג בַּעֲבֹתִים עַד קַרְנוֹת הַמִּזְבֵּחַ.
אֵל יְהֹוָה וַיָּאֶר לָנוּ,
אִסְרוּ חַג בַּעֲבֹתִים עַד קַרְנוֹת הַמִּזְבֵּחַ.

For a transliteration of the following text, please turn to page 174.

אֵלִי אַתָּה וְאוֹדֶךָּ,
אֱלֹהַי אֲרוֹמְמֶךָּ.
אֵלִי אַתָּה וְאוֹדֶךָּ,
אֱלֹהַי אֲרוֹמְמֶךָּ.

הוֹדוּ לַיהֹוָה כִּי טוֹב,
כִּי לְעוֹלָם חַסְדּוֹ.
הוֹדוּ לַיהֹוָה כִּי טוֹב,
כִּי לְעוֹלָם חַסְדּוֹ.

יְהַלְלוּךָ יְהֹוָה אֱלֹהֵינוּ כָּל מַעֲשֶׂיךָ,
וַחֲסִידֶיךָ צַדִּיקִים עוֹשֵׂי רְצוֹנֶךָ,
וְכָל עַמְּךָ בֵּית יִשְׂרָאֵל, בְּרִנָּה יוֹדוּ וִיבָרְכוּ,
וִישַׁבְּחוּ וִיפָאֲרוּ וִירוֹמְמוּ וְיַעֲרִיצוּ,
וְיַקְדִּישׁוּ וְיַמְלִיכוּ אֶת שִׁמְךָ, מַלְכֵּנוּ.
כִּי לְךָ טוֹב לְהוֹדוֹת וּלְשִׁמְךָ נָאֶה לְזַמֵּר,
כִּי מֵעוֹלָם וְעַד עוֹלָם אַתָּה אֵל.

הוֹדוּ לַיהֹוָה כִּי טוֹב, כִּי לְעוֹלָם חַסְדּוֹ.
הוֹדוּ לֵאלֹהֵי הָאֱלֹהִים, כִּי לְעוֹלָם חַסְדּוֹ.
הוֹדוּ לַאֲדֹנֵי הָאֲדֹנִים, כִּי לְעוֹלָם חַסְדּוֹ.
לְעֹשֵׂה נִפְלָאוֹת גְּדֹלוֹת לְבַדּוֹ, כִּי לְעוֹלָם חַסְדּוֹ.
לְעֹשֵׂה הַשָּׁמַיִם בִּתְבוּנָה, כִּי לְעוֹלָם חַסְדּוֹ.
לְרֹקַע הָאָרֶץ עַל הַמָּיִם, כִּי לְעוֹלָם חַסְדּוֹ.

Who made the great lights,	for His kindness is everlasting.
The sun to rule by day,	for His kindness is everlasting.
The moon and stars to rule by night,	for His kindness is everlasting.
Who struck Egypt through their firstborn,	for His kindness is everlasting.
And brought Israel out of their midst	for His kindness is everlasting.
With a strong hand and with an outstretched arm,	for His kindness is everlasting.
Who split the Sea of Reeds into parts,	for His kindness is everlasting.
And led Israel through it,	for His kindness is everlasting.
And cast Pharaoh and his army into the Sea of Reeds,	for His kindness is everlasting.
Who led His people through the desert,	for His kindness is everlasting.
Who struck great kings,	for His kindness is everlasting.
And slew mighty kings,	for His kindness is everlasting.
Sichon, king of the Amorites,	for His kindness is everlasting.
And Og, king of Bashan,	for His kindness is everlasting.
And gave their land as a heritage,	for His kindness is everlasting.
A heritage to Israel, His servant,	for His kindness is everlasting.
Who in our lowliness remembered us,	for His kindness is everlasting.
And delivered us from our oppressors,	for His kindness is everlasting.
Who gives bread to all flesh,	for His kindness is everlasting.
Thank the Almighty God of heaven,	for His kindness is everlasting.

The soul of every living being shall bless Your Name, Lord, our God.
And the spirit of all flesh
shall always glorify and exalt Your remembrance, our King.
From the beginning until the end of time, You are Almighty God,
and other than You, we have no King, Redeemer and Savior
who delivers, rescues, sustains, and is merciful in every time of trouble and distress.
We have no King but You.
[You are] the God of the first and of the last, God of all creatures,
Master of all events, who is extolled with a multitude of praises,
who directs His world with kindness and His creations with compassion.
And the Lord neither slumbers nor sleeps.
He arouses the sleepers and awakens the slumberers,

לְעֹשֵׂה אוֹרִים גְּדֹלִים, כִּי לְעוֹלָם חַסְדּוֹ.
אֶת הַשֶּׁמֶשׁ לְמֶמְשֶׁלֶת בַּיּוֹם, כִּי לְעוֹלָם חַסְדּוֹ.
אֶת הַיָּרֵחַ וְכוֹכָבִים לְמֶמְשְׁלוֹת בַּלָּיְלָה, כִּי לְעוֹלָם חַסְדּוֹ.
לְמַכֵּה מִצְרַיִם בִּבְכוֹרֵיהֶם, כִּי לְעוֹלָם חַסְדּוֹ.
וַיּוֹצֵא יִשְׂרָאֵל מִתּוֹכָם, כִּי לְעוֹלָם חַסְדּוֹ.
בְּיָד חֲזָקָה וּבִזְרוֹעַ נְטוּיָה, כִּי לְעוֹלָם חַסְדּוֹ.
לְגֹזֵר יַם סוּף לִגְזָרִים, כִּי לְעוֹלָם חַסְדּוֹ.
וְהֶעֱבִיר יִשְׂרָאֵל בְּתוֹכוֹ, כִּי לְעוֹלָם חַסְדּוֹ.
וְנִעֵר פַּרְעֹה וְחֵילוֹ בְיַם סוּף, כִּי לְעוֹלָם חַסְדּוֹ.
לְמוֹלִיךְ עַמּוֹ בַּמִּדְבָּר, כִּי לְעוֹלָם חַסְדּוֹ.
לְמַכֵּה מְלָכִים גְּדֹלִים, כִּי לְעוֹלָם חַסְדּוֹ.
וַיַּהֲרֹג מְלָכִים אַדִּירִים, כִּי לְעוֹלָם חַסְדּוֹ.
לְסִיחוֹן מֶלֶךְ הָאֱמֹרִי, כִּי לְעוֹלָם חַסְדּוֹ.
וּלְעוֹג מֶלֶךְ הַבָּשָׁן, כִּי לְעוֹלָם חַסְדּוֹ.
וְנָתַן אַרְצָם לְנַחֲלָה, כִּי לְעוֹלָם חַסְדּוֹ.
נַחֲלָה לְיִשְׂרָאֵל עַבְדּוֹ, כִּי לְעוֹלָם חַסְדּוֹ.
שֶׁבְּשִׁפְלֵנוּ זָכַר לָנוּ, כִּי לְעוֹלָם חַסְדּוֹ.
וַיִּפְרְקֵנוּ מִצָּרֵינוּ, כִּי לְעוֹלָם חַסְדּוֹ.
נֹתֵן לֶחֶם לְכָל בָּשָׂר, כִּי לְעוֹלָם חַסְדּוֹ.
הוֹדוּ לְאֵל הַשָּׁמָיִם, כִּי לְעוֹלָם חַסְדּוֹ.

נִשְׁמַת כָּל חַי תְּבָרֵךְ אֶת שִׁמְךָ יְהֹוָה אֱלֹהֵינוּ.
וְרוּחַ כָּל בָּשָׂר
תְּפָאֵר וּתְרוֹמֵם זִכְרְךָ מַלְכֵּנוּ תָּמִיד.
מִן הָעוֹלָם וְעַד הָעוֹלָם אַתָּה אֵל,
וּמִבַּלְעָדֶיךָ אֵין לָנוּ מֶלֶךְ גּוֹאֵל וּמוֹשִׁיעַ,
פּוֹדֶה וּמַצִּיל וּמְפַרְנֵס וּמְרַחֵם בְּכָל עֵת צָרָה וְצוּקָה.
אֵין לָנוּ מֶלֶךְ אֶלָּא אָתָּה.
אֱלֹהֵי הָרִאשׁוֹנִים וְהָאַחֲרוֹנִים, אֱלוֹהַּ כָּל בְּרִיּוֹת,
אֲדוֹן כָּל תּוֹלָדוֹת, הַמְּהֻלָּל בְּרֹב הַתִּשְׁבָּחוֹת,
הַמְנַהֵג עוֹלָמוֹ בְּחֶסֶד וּבְרִיּוֹתָיו בְּרַחֲמִים.
וַיהֹוָה עֵר הִנֵּה לֹא יָנוּם וְלֹא יִישָׁן.
הַמְעוֹרֵר יְשֵׁנִים וְהַמֵּקִיץ נִרְדָּמִים,

gives speech to the mute, releases those in bondage,
and supports the fallen, and raises up those who are bowed down.
To You alone we give thanks.

---

words, *Nishmat Kol Chai*, "the soul of every living being". This is the blessing that concludes *Pesukei D'zimrah* during the morning service on both Shabbat and the festivals. According to Rabbi Shmuel ben Meir, the grandson of Rashi, a leading French Tosafist in the 12th century CE, it is called the Blessing of the Song because it is a long and beautiful song of praise. It is therefore an appropriate conclusion to *Hallel*, the most special prayer of thanksgiving in Jewish liturgy.

Even if our mouths were filled with song as the sea,
and our tongues with [songs of] joy like the multitudes of its waves,
and our lips with praise like the expanse of the firmament,
and our eyes shining like the sun and the moon,
and our hands spread out like the eagles of the sky,
and our feet swift like deer,
we would still be unable to sufficiently thank You,
Lord, our God, and God of our forefathers,
and to bless Your Name,
for even one of the thousand of thousands upon thousands,
and myriads of myriads of instances of favors
that You have done for our ancestors and for us.
From Egypt, You have redeemed us, Lord, our God,
and from the house of bondage you have freed us,
in [times of] famine, you have fed us,
and in [times of] plenty you have supported us,
from the sword you have saved us,
and from pestilence you have delivered us,
and spared us from evil and lasting maladies.

Until now Your mercies have helped us,
and Your kindness has not forsaken us,
and may You not abandon us, Lord, our God, for eternity.
Therefore, the limbs which You have arranged within us,

הַמַּשִּׂיחַ אִלְּמִים וְהַמַּתִּיר אֲסוּרִים,
וְהַסּוֹמֵךְ נוֹפְלִים וְהַזּוֹקֵף כְּפוּפִים.
לְךָ לְבַדְּךָ אֲנַחְנוּ מוֹדִים.

Q&A

Why is "*Nishmat Kol Chai*" part of Hallel?

The Mishnah, in *Pesachim* 118a, states that following *Birkat Ha'Mazon* and the drinking of the third cup, the fourth cup is poured, and then *Hallel* is recited along with the "Blessing of the Song". The Gemara then records a debate over what exactly is the "Blessing of the Song". Rabbi Yochanan's opinion, which has been adopted and incorporated in the *Haggadah*, is that it is the blessing that begins with the

---

אִלּוּ פִינוּ מָלֵא שִׁירָה כַּיָּם,
וּלְשׁוֹנֵנוּ רִנָּה כַּהֲמוֹן גַּלָּיו,
וְשִׂפְתוֹתֵינוּ שֶׁבַח כְּמֶרְחֲבֵי רָקִיעַ,
מְאִירוֹת כַּשֶּׁמֶשׁ וְכַיָּרֵחַ,
וְיָדֵינוּ פְרוּשׂוֹת כְּנִשְׁרֵי שָׁמָיִם,
וְרַגְלֵינוּ קַלּוֹת כָּאַיָּלוֹת,
אֵין אֲנַחְנוּ מַסְפִּיקִים לְהוֹדוֹת לְךָ,
יְהֹוָה אֱלֹהֵינוּ וֵאלֹהֵי אֲבוֹתֵינוּ,
וּלְבָרֵךְ אֶת שְׁמֶךָ,
עַל אַחַת מֵאֶלֶף אַלְפֵי אֲלָפִים,
וְרִבֵּי רְבָבוֹת פְּעָמִים הַטּוֹבוֹת
שֶׁעָשִׂיתָ עִם אֲבוֹתֵינוּ וְעִמָּנוּ.
מִמִּצְרַיִם גְּאַלְתָּנוּ, יְהֹוָה אֱלֹהֵינוּ,
וּמִבֵּית עֲבָדִים פְּדִיתָנוּ,
בְּרָעָב זַנְתָּנוּ,
וּבְשָׂבָע כִּלְכַּלְתָּנוּ,
מֵחֶרֶב הִצַּלְתָּנוּ,
וּמִדֶּבֶר מִלַּטְתָּנוּ,
וּמֵחֳלָיִם רָעִים וְנֶאֱמָנִים דִּלִּיתָנוּ.

עַד הֵנָּה עֲזָרוּנוּ רַחֲמֶיךָ,
וְלֹא עֲזָבוּנוּ חֲסָדֶיךָ,
וְאַל תִּטְּשֵׁנוּ, יְהֹוָה אֱלֹהֵינוּ, לָנֶצַח.
עַל כֵּן אֵבָרִים שֶׁפִּלַּגְתָּ בָּנוּ,

and the spirit and soul which You have breathed into our nostrils,
and the tongue which You have placed in our mouth—
they all shall thank, and bless, and praise, and glorify,
and exalt, and adore, and sanctify, and proclaim the sovereignty
of Your Name, our King.
For every mouth shall offer thanks to You,
and every tongue shall swear allegiance by You,
and every knee shall bend to You,
and all who stand upright shall bow down before You,
and all hearts shall be in awe of You,
and all that is within us shall sing praise to Your Name,
as it is written:
"All my bones will say: Lord, who is like You?
You save the poor from one stronger than he,
and the poor and the needy from one who would rob him!"
Who is like You? Who is equal to You?
Who is comparable to You?
O great, mighty, awesome Almighty God, God most high, maker of heaven and earth!
We will praise You, extoll You and glorify You, and we will bless Your holy Name,
as it is said:
"[A Psalm] by David; bless the Lord, O my soul,
and all that is within me [bless] His holy Name."

The Almighty God, in the power of Your strength,
the Great One, in the glory of Your Name,
the Mighty One, for eternity,
and the Awesome One, in Your awesome deeds,
the King, who sits upon a throne,
high and exalted.
He who dwells for eternity,
lofty and holy is His Name.
And it is written:
"Righteous ones, sing joyously to the Lord,
it befits the upright to offer praise."

וְרוּחַ וּנְשָׁמָה שֶׁנָּפַחְתָּ בְּאַפֵּנוּ,
וְלָשׁוֹן אֲשֶׁר שַׂמְתָּ בְּפִינוּ–
הֵן הֵם יוֹדוּ וִיבָרְכוּ וִישַׁבְּחוּ וִיפָאֲרוּ
וִירוֹמְמוּ וְיַעֲרִיצוּ וְיַקְדִּישׁוּ וְיַמְלִיכוּ
אֶת שִׁמְךָ מַלְכֵּנוּ.
כִּי כָל פֶּה לְךָ יוֹדֶה,
וְכָל לָשׁוֹן לְךָ תִּשָּׁבַע,
וְכָל בֶּרֶךְ לְךָ תִכְרַע,
וְכָל קוֹמָה לְפָנֶיךָ תִשְׁתַּחֲוֶה,
וְכָל לְבָבוֹת יִירָאוּךָ,
וְכָל קֶרֶב וּכְלָיוֹת יְזַמְּרוּ לִשְׁמֶךָ,
כַּדָּבָר שֶׁכָּתוּב:
כָּל עַצְמֹתַי תֹּאמַרְנָה, יְהֹוָה מִי כָמוֹךָ?
מַצִּיל עָנִי מֵחָזָק מִמֶּנּוּ,
וְעָנִי וְאֶבְיוֹן מִגֹּזְלוֹ.
מִי יִדְמֶה לָּךְ? וּמִי יִשְׁוֶה לָּךְ?
וּמִי יַעֲרָךְ לָךְ?
הָאֵל הַגָּדוֹל, הַגִּבּוֹר וְהַנּוֹרָא, אֵל עֶלְיוֹן, קֹנֵה שָׁמַיִם וָאָרֶץ!
נְהַלֶּלְךָ וּנְשַׁבֵּחֲךָ וּנְפָאֶרְךָ וּנְבָרֵךְ אֶת שֵׁם קָדְשֶׁךָ,
כָּאָמוּר:
לְדָוִד, בָּרְכִי נַפְשִׁי אֶת יְהֹוָה
וְכָל קְרָבַי אֶת שֵׁם קָדְשׁוֹ.

הָאֵל בְּתַעֲצֻמוֹת עֻזֶּךָ,
הַגָּדוֹל בִּכְבוֹד שְׁמֶךָ,
הַגִּבּוֹר לָנֶצַח,
וְהַנּוֹרָא בְּנוֹרְאוֹתֶיךָ,
הַמֶּלֶךְ הַיּוֹשֵׁב עַל כִּסֵּא,
רָם וְנִשָּׂא.
שׁוֹכֵן עַד,
מָרוֹם וְקָדוֹשׁ שְׁמוֹ.
וְכָתוּב:
רַנְּנוּ צַדִּיקִים בַּיהֹוָה,
לַיְשָׁרִים נָאוָה תְהִלָּה.

By the mouth of the upright You are praised.
And by the words of the righteous You are blessed.
And by the tongue of the pious You are exalted.
And among the holy ones You are sanctified.

In the assemblies of the myriads of Your people, the House of Israel,
in [songs of] joy Your Name, our King, shall be glorified in every generation.
For this is the obligation of all creatures before You,
Lord, our God, and God of our forefathers,
to thank, to praise, to laud, to glorify, to exalt,
to honor, to bless, to raise up high, and to acclaim [You],
even beyond all the words of songs and praises
of David, son of Yishai, Your anointed servant.

[Therefore,] **May Your Name be praised** forever, our King,
the Almighty God, the King, the Great One,
and the Holy One in heaven and on earth.
For to You, it befits to offer, Lord, our God and God of our forefathers,
song and praise, hymn and song, strength and dominion,
victory, greatness and might, praise and glory,
holiness and sovereignty, blessings and thanks
from now until the end of time.
Blessed are You, Lord, Almighty God, great King, extolled in praises,
Almighty God of thanksgivings, Master of wonders,
who takes pleasure in hymns of song,
King, Almighty God, the Life of all worlds.

Recite the blessing for the wine, and drink in reclining position.

Blessed are You, Lord, our God, King of the universe,
who creates the fruit of the vine.

בְּפִי יְשָׁרִים	תִּתְהַלָּל.
וּבְדִבְרֵי צַדִּיקִים	תִּתְבָּרַךְ.
וּבִלְשׁוֹן חֲסִידִים	תִּתְרוֹמָם.
וּבְקֶרֶב קְדוֹשִׁים	תִּתְקַדָּשׁ.

וּבְמַקְהֲלוֹת רִבְבוֹת עַמְּךָ בֵּית יִשְׂרָאֵל,
בְּרִנָּה יִתְפָּאַר שִׁמְךָ, מַלְכֵּנוּ, בְּכָל דּוֹר וָדוֹר.
שֶׁכֵּן חוֹבַת כָּל הַיְצוּרִים לְפָנֶיךָ,
יְהֹוָה אֱלֹהֵינוּ וֵאלֹהֵי אֲבוֹתֵינוּ,
לְהוֹדוֹת, לְהַלֵּל, לְשַׁבֵּחַ, לְפָאֵר, לְרוֹמֵם,
לְהַדֵּר, לְבָרֵךְ, לְעַלֵּה וּלְקַלֵּס,
עַל כָּל דִּבְרֵי שִׁירוֹת וְתִשְׁבְּחוֹת
דָּוִד בֶּן יִשַׁי, עַבְדְּךָ מְשִׁיחֶךָ.

יִשְׁתַּבַּח שִׁמְךָ לָעַד מַלְכֵּנוּ,
הָאֵל הַמֶּלֶךְ הַגָּדוֹל,
וְהַקָּדוֹשׁ בַּשָּׁמַיִם וּבָאָרֶץ.
כִּי לְךָ נָאֶה יְהֹוָה אֱלֹהֵינוּ וֵאלֹהֵי אֲבוֹתֵינוּ,
שִׁיר וּשְׁבָחָה, הַלֵּל וְזִמְרָה, עֹז וּמֶמְשָׁלָה,
נֶצַח, גְּדֻלָּה וּגְבוּרָה, תְּהִלָּה וְתִפְאֶרֶת,
קְדֻשָּׁה וּמַלְכוּת, בְּרָכוֹת וְהוֹדָאוֹת
מֵעַתָּה וְעַד עוֹלָם.
בָּרוּךְ אַתָּה יְהֹוָה, אֵל מֶלֶךְ גָּדוֹל בַּתִּשְׁבָּחוֹת,
אֵל הַהוֹדָאוֹת, אֲדוֹן הַנִּפְלָאוֹת,
הַבּוֹחֵר בְּשִׁירֵי זִמְרָה,
מֶלֶךְ אֵל חֵי הָעוֹלָמִים.

Recite the ברכה for the wine, and drink in reclining position.

בָּרוּךְ אַתָּה יְהֹוָה אֱלֹהֵינוּ מֶלֶךְ הָעוֹלָם,
בּוֹרֵא פְּרִי הַגָּפֶן.

The After-Blessing

The following blessing is said after drinking the fourth and last cup of wine.
Do not drink any more wine, after saying the blessing.

Blessed are You, Lord, our God, King of the universe,
for the vine and the fruit of the vine, and for the produce of the field,
for the desirable, good and spacious land
that You willingly gave as a heritage to our ancestors,
that they might eat of its fruit and be satisfied with its goodness.
Have compassion, Lord, our God, on Israel, Your people,
and on Jerusalem, Your city, on Zion, the home of Your glory,
and on Your altar and on Your Temple.
And may You rebuild Jerusalem, the holy city, swiftly in our days,
and may You bring us back there, rejoicing in its rebuilding,
and we shall eat from its fruit, satisfied by its goodness,
and we shall bless You for it, in holiness and purity.

On Shabbat add:

Be pleased to refresh us on this Sabbath day.

Grant us joy on this festival of Matzot.
For You, Lord, are good and do good to all,
and we thank You for the land and for the fruit of the vine.
Blessed are You, Lord, for the land and for the fruit of the vine.

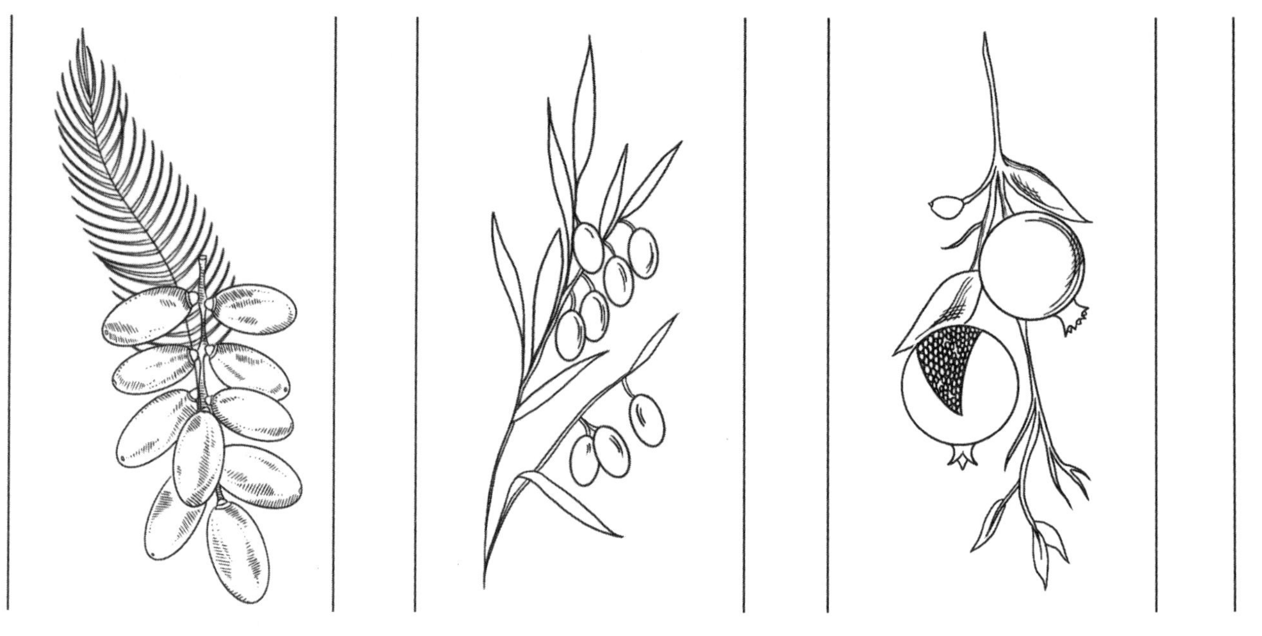

ברכה אחרונה

The following ברכה is said after drinking the fourth and last cup of wine.
Do not drink any more wine, after saying the ברכה.

בָּרוּךְ אַתָּה יְהֹוָה אֱלֹהֵינוּ מֶלֶךְ הָעוֹלָם,
עַל הַגֶּפֶן וְעַל פְּרִי הַגֶּפֶן וְעַל תְּנוּבַת הַשָּׂדֶה,
וְעַל אֶרֶץ חֶמְדָּה טוֹבָה וּרְחָבָה
שֶׁרָצִיתָ וְהִנְחַלְתָּ לַאֲבוֹתֵינוּ.
לֶאֱכֹל מִפִּרְיָהּ וְלִשְׂבֹּעַ מִטּוּבָהּ.
רַחֵם נָא יְהֹוָה אֱלֹהֵינוּ עַל יִשְׂרָאֵל עַמֶּךָ.
וְעַל יְרוּשָׁלַיִם עִירֶךָ, וְעַל צִיּוֹן מִשְׁכַּן כְּבוֹדֶךָ.
וְעַל מִזְבְּחֶךָ וְעַל הֵיכָלֶךָ.
וּבְנֵה יְרוּשָׁלַיִם עִיר הַקֹּדֶשׁ בִּמְהֵרָה בְיָמֵינוּ,
וְהַעֲלֵנוּ לְתוֹכָהּ, וְשַׂמְּחֵנוּ בְּבִנְיָנָהּ,
וְנֹאכַל מִפִּרְיָהּ וְנִשְׂבַּע מִטּוּבָהּ,
וּנְבָרֶכְךָ עָלֶיהָ בִּקְדֻשָּׁה וּבְטָהֳרָה.

On שבת add:

וּרְצֵה וְהַחֲלִיצֵנוּ בְּיוֹם הַשַּׁבָּת הַזֶּה.

וְשַׂמְּחֵנוּ בְּיוֹם חַג הַמַּצּוֹת הַזֶּה.
כִּי אַתָּה יְהֹוָה טוֹב וּמֵטִיב לַכֹּל,
וְנוֹדֶה לְּךָ עַל הָאָרֶץ וְעַל פְּרִי הַגָּפֶן.
בָּרוּךְ אַתָּה יְהֹוָה, עַל הָאָרֶץ וְעַל פְּרִי הַגָּפֶן.

NIRTZAH
THE CONCLUSION

The Pesach service is finished, as it was meant to be performed,
in accordance with all its rules and laws.
Just as we have been privileged to lay out its order,
so may we be privileged to perform it [in the Temple].
Pure One, dwelling in the habitation,
raise up this people, too abundant to be counted.
Soon, lead the shoots of [Israel's] stock, redeemed, into Zion with [songs of] joy.

Next Year in Jerusalem Rebuilt!

נרצה

חֲסַל סִדּוּר פֶּסַח כְּהִלְכָתוֹ,
כְּכָל מִשְׁפָּטוֹ וְחֻקָּתוֹ.
כַּאֲשֶׁר זָכִינוּ לְסַדֵּר אוֹתוֹ,
כֵּן נִזְכֶּה לַעֲשׂוֹתוֹ.
זָךְ שׁוֹכֵן מְעוֹנָה,
קוֹמֵם קְהַל עֲדַת מִי מָנָה.
בְּקָרוֹב נַהֵל נִטְעֵי כַנָּה, פְּדוּיִם לְצִיּוֹן בְּרִנָּה.

לְשָׁנָה הַבָּאָה בִּירוּשָׁלָיִם הַבְּנוּיָה!

When do we say, “Next year in Jerusalem rebuilt” at the end of another holiday?

The only other festival that ends with the statement, “Next year in Jerusalem” is Yom Kippur.

Why do we say, “Next year in Jerusalem rebuilt”, at the end of the *seder*?

The *seder* begins with the statement, ”Now we are here; next year in the land of Israel”. The *seder* therefore comes full circle, with the central hope of Jews throughout history: that we will be in our own land. Yearning to be in the land of Zion is of ancient vintage. The exiles on the road to Babylon lamented, “How can we sing the Lord’s song on foreign soil? If I forget you, O Jerusalem, may my right hand forget its skill, may my tongue cling to the roof of my mouth, if I do not remember you, if I do not set Jerusalem above my highest joy.” Longing for Jerusalem, and the Land of Israel, is a central component of our daily prayers, as we recite during the morning, afternoon and evening *Amidah* a prayer not only to return to Israel (“Blow the great shofar for our freedom, and carry the banner to gather the exiles, and gather us from the four corners of the earth . . .”), but also that Jerusalem be rebuilt (“And to Jerusalem, Your city, may You return, and dwell within it, as You have spoken, and build it soon, in our days . . .”). We end the *seder* where we started, as if to say that although we have journeyed from slavery to freedom, our ultimate redemption has not yet been accomplished. We are no longer slaves of Pharaoh, and although we are free, and even possess the land of Israel itself, the transformation is not complete until Jerusalem is rebuilt. Jerusalem may be the shining, modern capital of the Jewish state of Israel, but God’s Kingship is not yet established without the Temple. Until that time, we must continue to pray – from the beginning until the end – to be in Jerusalem rebuilt.

SEDER NIGHT SONGS

He is Mighty

He is Mighty!
May He rebuild His house soon,
quickly, quickly in our days soon.
O Almighty God, rebuild it! O Almighty God, rebuild it! Rebuild your house soon,

He is chosen, He is great, He is lofty! May He rebuild His house soon...

He is splendid, He is distinguished, He is commendable, May He rebuild His house soon...

He is pious, He is pure, He is unique! May He rebuild His house soon...

He is powerful, He is learned, He is sovereign! May He rebuild His house soon...

He is awesome, He is mighty, He is powerful! May He rebuild His house soon...

He is a redeemer, He is righteous, He is holy! May He rebuild His house soon...

He is merciful, He is [known as] Shaddai, He is resolute! May He rebuild His house soon...

What is the meaning of this song?

When a language has many words that are synonyms for the same idea, this may suggest that the idea is important within that language. For example, in Eskimo–Aleut, there are many synonyms for the word "snow" (although 50 synonyms is more myth than fact). In contrast, Hebrew has many synonyms for the word "praise". Just as in *Hallel* we praise God during the *seder*, the first song we sing following the *seder* is one of praise. *Adir Hu*, written as an acrostic, describes the many divine attributes of God. Given that we ended the liturgy of the *Haggadah* with the hope that we will be "Next year in Jerusalem rebuilt", it is fitting that our lavish praises in *Adir Hu* call on Him to fulfill that hope through the rebuilding of His "home", the Temple, quickly, quickly, in our days soon!

שירי ליל הסדר

אדיר הוא

אַדִּיר הוּא!
יִבְנֶה בֵּיתוֹ בְּקָרוֹב,
בִּמְהֵרָה בִּמְהֵרָה, בְּיָמֵינוּ בְּקָרוֹב.
אֵל בְּנֵה, אֵל בְּנֵה, בְּנֵה בֵּיתְךָ בְּקָרוֹב.

בָּחוּר הוּא, גָּדוֹל הוּא, דָּגוּל הוּא! יִבְנֶה בֵּיתוֹ בְּקָרוֹב...

הָדוּר הוּא, וָתִיק הוּא, זַכַּאי הוּא! יִבְנֶה בֵּיתוֹ בְּקָרוֹב...

חָסִיד הוּא, טָהוֹר הוּא, יָחִיד הוּא! יִבְנֶה בֵּיתוֹ בְּקָרוֹב...

כַּבִּיר הוּא, לָמוּד הוּא, מֶלֶךְ הוּא! יִבְנֶה בֵּיתוֹ בְּקָרוֹב...

נוֹרָא הוּא, סַגִּיב הוּא, עִזּוּז הוּא! יִבְנֶה בֵּיתוֹ בְּקָרוֹב...

פּוֹדֶה הוּא, צַדִּיק הוּא, קָדוֹשׁ הוּא! יִבְנֶה בֵּיתוֹ בְּקָרוֹב...

רַחוּם הוּא, שַׁדַּי הוּא, תַּקִּיף הוּא! יִבְנֶה בֵּיתוֹ בְּקָרוֹב...

Q&A

What is the symbolic meaning of an acrostic poem in Judaism?

Acrostic poems are poems where the first letter of each word, line or stanza proceed from the first to last letters of the alphabet or spell out a message or name. This is a common writing style in Jewish poetry. Among the well-known acrostic poems are *Eshet Chayil*, where the first letter of each line proceeds from *aleph* to *tav*, and *Yah Ribon Olam*, the first letter of which spells out the name of the author, Yitzhak Luria Chazak. Acrostic poems in which the first letter of each word, line or stanza proceed from *aleph* to *tav* suggest the idea of completeness.

Who Knows One?

Who knows one? I know one!
One is our God in heaven and on the earth.

Who knows two? I know two!
Two are the tablets of the covenant.
One is our God in heaven and on the earth.

Who knows three? I know three!
Three are our forefathers.
Two are the tablets of the covenant.
One is our God in heaven and on the earth.

Who knows four? I know four!
Four are our matriarchs.
Three are our forefathers.
Two are the tablets of the covenant.
One is our God in heaven and on the earth.

Who knows five? I know five!
Five are the books of the Torah.
Four are our matriarchs.
Three are our forefathers.
Two are the tablets of the covenant.
One is our God in heaven and on the earth.

Who knows six? I know six!
Six are the orders of the Mishna.
Five are the books of the Torah.
Four are our matriarchs.
Three are our forefathers.
Two are the tablets of the covenant.
One is our God in heaven and on the earth.
Who knows seven? I know seven!

אחד מי יודע

אֶחָד מִי יוֹדֵעַ? אֶחָד אֲנִי יוֹדֵעַ!
אֶחָד אֱלֹהֵינוּ שֶׁבַּשָּׁמַיִם וּבָאָרֶץ.

שְׁנַיִם מִי יוֹדֵעַ? שְׁנַיִם אֲנִי יוֹדֵעַ!
שְׁנֵי לֻחוֹת הַבְּרִית.
אֶחָד אֱלֹהֵינוּ שֶׁבַּשָּׁמַיִם וּבָאָרֶץ.

שְׁלֹשָׁה מִי יוֹדֵעַ? שְׁלֹשָׁה אֲנִי יוֹדֵעַ!
שְׁלֹשָׁה אָבוֹת.
שְׁנֵי לֻחוֹת הַבְּרִית.
אֶחָד אֱלֹהֵינוּ שֶׁבַּשָּׁמַיִם וּבָאָרֶץ.

אַרְבַּע מִי יוֹדֵעַ? אַרְבַּע אֲנִי יוֹדֵעַ!
אַרְבַּע אִמָּהוֹת.
שְׁלֹשָׁה אָבוֹת.
שְׁנֵי לֻחוֹת הַבְּרִית.
אֶחָד אֱלֹהֵינוּ שֶׁבַּשָּׁמַיִם וּבָאָרֶץ.

חֲמִשָּׁה מִי יוֹדֵעַ? חֲמִשָּׁה אֲנִי יוֹדֵעַ!
חֲמִשָּׁה חוּמְשֵׁי תוֹרָה.
אַרְבַּע אִמָּהוֹת.
שְׁלֹשָׁה אָבוֹת.
שְׁנֵי לֻחוֹת הַבְּרִית.
אֶחָד אֱלֹהֵינוּ שֶׁבַּשָּׁמַיִם וּבָאָרֶץ.

שִׁשָּׁה מִי יוֹדֵעַ? שִׁשָּׁה אֲנִי יוֹדֵעַ!
שִׁשָּׁה סִדְרֵי מִשְׁנָה.
חֲמִשָּׁה חוּמְשֵׁי תוֹרָה.
אַרְבַּע אִמָּהוֹת.
שְׁלֹשָׁה אָבוֹת.
שְׁנֵי לֻחוֹת הַבְּרִית.
אֶחָד אֱלֹהֵינוּ שֶׁבַּשָּׁמַיִם וּבָאָרֶץ.
שִׁבְעָה מִי יוֹדֵעַ? שִׁבְעָה אֲנִי יוֹדֵעַ!

Seven are the days [from Shabbat] to Shabbat.
Six are the orders of the Mishna.
Five are the books of the Torah.
Four are our matriarchs.
Three are our forefathers.
Two are the tablets of the covenant.
One is our God in heaven and on the earth.

Who knows eight? I know eight!
Eight are the days to a brit.
Seven are the days [from Shabbat] to Shabbat.
Six are the orders of the Mishna.
Five are the books of the Torah.
Four are our matriarchs.
Three are our forefathers.
Two are the tablets of the covenant.
One is our God in heaven and on the earth.

Who knows nine? I know nine!
Nine are the months until birth.
Eight are the days to a brit.
Seven are the days [from Shabbat] to Shabbat.
Six are the orders of the Mishna.
Five are the books of the Torah.
Four are our matriarchs.
Three are our forefathers.
Two are the tablets of the covenant.
One is our God in heaven and on the earth.

Who knows ten? I know ten!
Ten are the [Ten] Commandments.
Nine are the months until birth.
Eight are the days to a brit.
Seven are the days [from Shabbat] to Shabbat.

שִׁבְעָה יְמֵי שַׁבַּתָּא.
שִׁשָּׁה סִדְרֵי מִשְׁנָה.
חֲמִשָּׁה חוּמְשֵׁי תוֹרָה.
אַרְבַּע אִמָּהוֹת.
שְׁלֹשָׁה אָבוֹת.
שְׁנֵי לֻחוֹת הַבְּרִית.
אֶחָד אֱלֹהֵינוּ שֶׁבַּשָּׁמַיִם וּבָאָרֶץ.

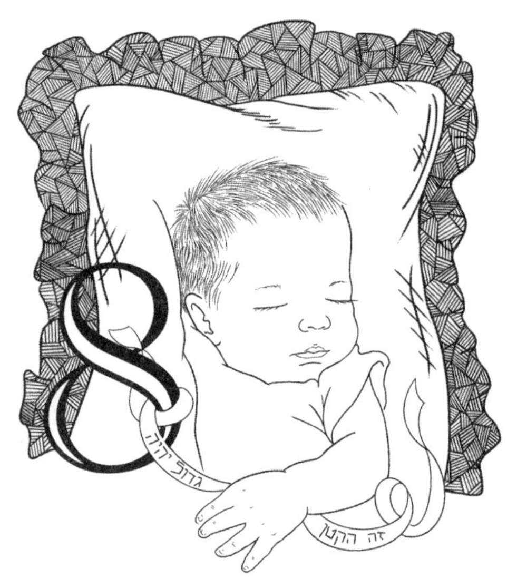

שְׁמוֹנָה מִי יוֹדֵעַ? שְׁמוֹנָה אֲנִי יוֹדֵעַ!
שְׁמוֹנָה יְמֵי מִילָה.
שִׁבְעָה יְמֵי שַׁבַּתָּא.
שִׁשָּׁה סִדְרֵי מִשְׁנָה.
חֲמִשָּׁה חוּמְשֵׁי תוֹרָה.
אַרְבַּע אִמָּהוֹת.
שְׁלֹשָׁה אָבוֹת.
שְׁנֵי לֻחוֹת הַבְּרִית.
אֶחָד אֱלֹהֵינוּ שֶׁבַּשָּׁמַיִם וּבָאָרֶץ.

תִּשְׁעָה מִי יוֹדֵעַ? תִּשְׁעָה אֲנִי יוֹדֵעַ!
תִּשְׁעָה יַרְחֵי לֵדָה.
שְׁמוֹנָה יְמֵי מִילָה.
שִׁבְעָה יְמֵי שַׁבַּתָּא.
שִׁשָּׁה סִדְרֵי מִשְׁנָה.
חֲמִשָּׁה חוּמְשֵׁי תוֹרָה.
אַרְבַּע אִמָּהוֹת.
שְׁלֹשָׁה אָבוֹת.
שְׁנֵי לֻחוֹת הַבְּרִית.
אֶחָד אֱלֹהֵינוּ שֶׁבַּשָּׁמַיִם וּבָאָרֶץ.

עֲשָׂרָה מִי יוֹדֵעַ? עֲשָׂרָה אֲנִי יוֹדֵעַ!
עֲשָׂרָה דִבְּרַיָּא.
תִּשְׁעָה יַרְחֵי לֵדָה.
שְׁמוֹנָה יְמֵי מִילָה.
שִׁבְעָה יְמֵי שַׁבַּתָּא.

Six are the orders of the Mishna.
Five are the books of the Torah.
Four are our matriarchs.
Three are our forefathers.
Two are the tablets of the covenant.
One is our God in heaven and on the earth.

Who knows eleven? I know eleven.
Eleven are the stars [in Joseph's dream].
Ten are the [Ten] Commandments.
Nine are the months until birth.
Eight are the days to a brit.
Seven are the days [from Shabbat] to Shabbat.
Six are the orders of the Mishna.
Five are the books of the Torah.
Four are our matriarchs.
Three are our forefathers.
Two are the tablets of the covenant.
One is our God in heaven and on the earth.

Who knows twelve? I know twelve.
Twelve are the [number of] tribes.
Eleven are the stars [in Joseph's dream].
Ten are the [Ten] Commandments.
Nine are the months until birth.
Eight are the days to a brit.
Seven are the days [from Shabbat] to Shabbat.
Six are the orders of the Mishna.
Five are the books of the Torah.
Four are our matriarchs.
Three are our forefathers.
Two are the tablets of the covenant.
One is our God in heaven and on the earth.

שִׁשָּׁה סִדְרֵי מִשְׁנָה.
חֲמִשָּׁה חוּמְשֵׁי תוֹרָה.
אַרְבַּע אִמָּהוֹת.
שְׁלשָׁה אָבוֹת.
שְׁנֵי לֻחוֹת הַבְּרִית.
אֶחָד אֱלֹהֵינוּ שֶׁבַּשָּׁמַיִם וּבָאָרֶץ.

אַחַד עָשָׂר מִי יוֹדֵעַ? אַחַד עָשָׂר אֲנִי יוֹדֵעַ!
אַחַד עָשָׂר כּוֹכְבַיָּא.
עֲשָׂרָה דִבְּרַיָּא.
תִּשְׁעָה יַרְחֵי לֵדָה.
שְׁמוֹנָה יְמֵי מִילָה.
שִׁבְעָה יְמֵי שַׁבַּתָּא.
שִׁשָּׁה סִדְרֵי מִשְׁנָה.
חֲמִשָּׁה חוּמְשֵׁי תוֹרָה.
אַרְבַּע אִמָּהוֹת.
שְׁלשָׁה אָבוֹת.
שְׁנֵי לֻחוֹת הַבְּרִית.
אֶחָד אֱלֹהֵינוּ שֶׁבַּשָּׁמַיִם וּבָאָרֶץ.

שְׁנֵים עָשָׂר מִי יוֹדֵעַ? שנים עָשָׂר אֲנִי יוֹדֵעַ!
שְׁנֵים עָשָׂר שִׁבְטַיָּא.
אַחַד עָשָׂר כּוֹכְבַיָּא.
עֲשָׂרָה דִבְּרַיָּא.
תִּשְׁעָה יַרְחֵי לֵדָה.
שְׁמוֹנָה יְמֵי מִילָה.
שִׁבְעָה יְמֵי שַׁבַּתָּא.
שִׁשָּׁה סִדְרֵי מִשְׁנָה.
חֲמִשָּׁה חוּמְשֵׁי תוֹרָה.
אַרְבַּע אִמָּהוֹת.
שְׁלשָׁה אָבוֹת.
שְׁנֵי לֻחוֹת הַבְּרִית.
אֶחָד אֱלֹהֵינוּ שֶׁבַּשָּׁמַיִם וּבָאָרֶץ.

Who knows thirteen? I know thirteen!
Thirteen are the attributes [of God's mercy].
Twelve are the [number of] tribes.
Eleven are the stars [in Joseph's dream].
Ten are the [Ten] Commandments.
Nine are the months until birth.
Eight are the days to a brit.
Seven are the days [from Shabbat] to Shabbat.
Six are the orders of the Mishna.
Five are the books of the Torah.
Four are our matriarchs.
Three are our forefathers.
Two are the tablets of the covenant.
One is our God in heaven and on the earth.

שְׁלֹשָׁה עָשָׂר מִי יוֹדֵעַ? שְׁלֹשָׁה עָשָׂר אֲנִי יוֹדֵעַ!
שְׁלֹשָׁה עָשָׂר מִדַּיָא.
שְׁנֵים עָשָׂר שִׁבְטַיָא.
אַחַד עָשָׂר כּוֹכְבַיָא.
עֲשָׂרָה דִבְּרַיָא.
תִּשְׁעָה יַרְחֵי לֵדָה.
שְׁמוֹנָה יְמֵי מִילָה.
שִׁבְעָה יְמֵי שַׁבַּתָא.
שִׁשָּׁה סִדְרֵי מִשְׁנָה.
חֲמִשָּׁה חוּמְשֵׁי תוֹרָה.
אַרְבַּע אִמָּהוֹת.
שְׁלֹשָׁה אָבוֹת.
שְׁנֵי לֻחוֹת הַבְּרִית.
אֶחָד אֱלֹהֵינוּ שֶׁבַּשָּׁמַיִם וּבָאָרֶץ.

What is the significance of the number thirteen?

The number 13 is related to the Thirteen Attributes of Mercy, *Shelosh-Esreh Middot HaRakhamim.* God taught Moses the Thirteen Attributes following the incident of the golden calf, when He threatened to destroy the Jewish people. The Thirteen Attributes describe the thirteen different manifestations of God's kindness, compassion and mercy to those who sin.

Why do we end the *seder* with this song?

The story of the Exodus begins with the thirteen plagues, because it was as a result of these miracles that Pharaoh freed the Jewish people. Thirteen plagues? While we normally think of ten plagues, Rabbi Yehuda grouped them together under three acronyms, *detzach, adash,* and *be'achav*, making thirteen. Upon saying each of these thirteen, we spill a drop of wine to signify our compassion for the Egyptians who suffered because of the plagues. Although the Egyptians visited great hardship upon the Jewish people, we take no joy in their suffering. The purpose of the Exodus was not to punish the Egyptians, but rather to free the Jewish people so that we could serve God. Yet, every Jew struggles in his service to God. Every Jew therefore needs God's divine mercy. That is what the Thirteen Attributes are for. Ending the *seder* with this song serves to remind us that just as God intervened to free us from Egypt with the plagues, he can continually redeem us through his mercy.

Chad Gadya

One little goat, one little goat, which my father bought for two zuzim.
One little goat, one little goat.

The cat came, and ate the goat, which my father bought for two zuzim.
One little goat, one little goat.

The dog came and bit the cat, that ate the goat, which my father bought for two zuzim.
One little goat, one little goat.

The stick came and beat the dog, that bit the cat, that ate the goat,
which my father bought for two zuzim.
One little goat, one little goat.

The fire came and burned the stick, that beat the dog, that bit the cat, that ate the goat,
which my father bought for two zuzim.
One little goat, one little goat.

The water came and put out the fire, that burned the stick, that beat the dog,
that bit the cat, that ate the goat,
which my father bought for two zuzim.
One little goat, one little goat.

The ox came and drank the water, that put out the fire, that burned the stick,
that beat the dog, that bit the cat, that ate the goat,
which my father bought for two zuzim.
One little goat, one little goat.

The slaughterer (shochet) came and killed the ox, that drank the water,
that put out the fire, that burned the stick, that beat the dog,
that bit the cat, that ate the goat,
which my father bought for two zuzim.
One little goat, one little goat.
The Angel of Death came and slew the slaughterer, who killed the ox,

חד גדיא

חַד גַּדְיָא, חַד גַּדְיָא דְּזַבִּין אַבָּא בִּתְרֵי זוּזֵי.
חַד גַּדְיָא, חַד גַּדְיָא.

וְאָתָא שׁוּנְרָא וְאָכְלָה לְגַדְיָא, דְּזַבִּין אַבָּא בִּתְרֵי זוּזֵי.
חַד גַּדְיָא, חַד גַּדְיָא.

וְאָתָא כַלְבָּא וְנָשַׁךְ לְשׁוּנְרָא, דְּאָכְלָה לְגַדְיָא, דְּזַבִּין אַבָּא בִּתְרֵי זוּזֵי.
חַד גַּדְיָא, חַד גַּדְיָא.

וְאָתָא חוּטְרָא והִכָּה לְכַלְבָּא, דְּנָשַׁךְ לְשׁוּנְרָא, דְּאָכְלָה לְגַדְיָא,
דְּזַבִּין אַבָּא בִּתְרֵי זוּזֵי.
חַד גַּדְיָא, חַד גַּדְיָא.

וְאָתָא נוּרָא וְשָׂרַף לְחוּטְרָא, דְּהִכָּה לְכַלְבָּא, דְּנָשַׁךְ לְשׁוּנְרָא, דְּאָכְלָה לְגַדְיָא,
דְּזַבִּין אַבָּא בִּתְרֵי זוּזֵי.
חַד גַּדְיָא, חַד גַּדְיָא.

וְאָתָא מַיָּא וְכָבָה לְנוּרָא, דְּשָׂרַף לְחוּטְרָא, דְּהִכָּה לְכַלְבָּא,
דְּנָשַׁךְ לְשׁוּנְרָא, דְּאָכְלָה לְגַדְיָא,
דְּזַבִּין אַבָּא בִּתְרֵי זוּזֵי.
חַד גַּדְיָא, חַד גַּדְיָא.

וְאָתָא תוֹרָא וְשָׁתָה לְמַיָּא, דְּכָבָה לְנוּרָא, דְּשָׂרַף לְחוּטְרָא,
דְּהִכָּה לְכַלְבָּא, דְּנָשַׁךְ לְשׁוּנְרָא, דְּאָכְלָה לְגַדְיָא,
דְּזַבִּין אַבָּא בִּתְרֵי זוּזֵי.
חַד גַּדְיָא, חַד גַּדְיָא.

וְאָתָא שׁוֹחֵט וְשָׁחַט לְתוֹרָא, דְּשָׁתָה לְמַיָּא,
דְּכָבָה לְנוּרָא, דְּשָׂרַף לְחוּטְרָא, דְּהִכָּה לְכַלְבָּא,
דְּנָשַׁךְ לְשׁוּנְרָא, דְּאָכְלָה לְגַדְיָא,
דְּזַבִּין אַבָּא בִּתְרֵי זוּזֵי.
חַד גַּדְיָא, חַד גַּדְיָא.
וְאָתָא מַלְאַךְ הַמָּוֶת וְשָׁחַט לְשׁוֹחֵט, דְּשָׁחַט לְתוֹרָא,

that drank the water, that put out the fire, that burned the stick,
that beat the dog, that bit the cat, that ate the goat,
which my father bought for two zuzim.
One little goat, one little goat.

The Holy One, blessed is He, came and smote the Angel of Death,
who slew the slaughterer, who killed the ox, that drank the water,
that put out the fire, that burned the stick, that beat the dog,
that bit the cat, that ate the goat,
which my father bought for two zuzim.
One little goat, one little goat.

---

step in the chain (the next being the dog, representing Anubis, the Egyptian god of the dead), the Egyptian sees other things to worship. However, the Jewish people see only the final actor, the one who is at the top of the food chain, so to speak, the Holy One, blessed is He! In yet another interpretation, the little lamb is the Jewish people, the cat is Egypt, the dog is Assyria and Babylon, the stick is Persia, and so on and so on, until ultimately the Holy One, blessed is He, demonstrates that He is above all earthly powers.

What do the two *zuzim* represent?

If the little lamb represents the Jewish people, then the two *zuzim* represent the two tablets of the Law, which the father – the Holy One, blessed is He – used to buy the lamb.

דְּשָׁתָה לְמַיָּא, דְּכָבָה לְנוּרָא, דְּשָׂרַף לְחוּטְרָא,
דְּהִכָּה לְכַלְבָּא, דְּנָשַׁךְ לְשׁוּנְרָא, דְּאָכְלָה לְגַדְיָא,
דְּזַבִּין אַבָּא בִּתְרֵי זוּזֵי.
חַד גַּדְיָא, חַד גַּדְיָא.

וְאָתָא הַקָּדוֹשׁ בָּרוּךְ הוּא וְשָׁחַט לְמַלְאַךְ הַמָּוֶת,
דְּשָׁחַט לְשׁוֹחֵט, דְּשָׁחַט לְתוֹרָא, דְּשָׁתָה לְמַיָּא,
דְּכָבָה לְנוּרָא, דְּשָׂרַף לְחוּטְרָא, דְּהִכָּה לְכַלְבָּא,
דְּנָשַׁךְ לְשׁוּנְרָא, דְּאָכְלָה לְגַדְיָא,
דְּזַבִּין אַבָּא בִּתְרֵי זוּזֵי.
חַד גַּדְיָא, חַד גַּדְיָא.

Q&A

What is the meaning of *Chad Gadya*?

There are numerous interpretations of this strange song. The simplest explanation is that the song is a fun way to end the *seder* that can stimulate the children to ask further questions. The song may also be seen as a parable – one that illustrates an important spiritual message. The "goat" is the Jewish people, tormented by a series of enemies. However, although enemies have arisen throughout our history, God is always there to avenge us and provide redemption, as symbolized by the smiting of the Angel of Death. Another interpretation is based on the fact that the Torah states that the sacrificial lamb may be taken from among the goats (Exodus 12:5). With this in mind, the goat can be seen as representative of the Egyptian god of the Nile source, Khnum, who had the head of a goat. An Egyptian sees the goat as something to worship. The goat is then eaten by a cat, which represents the Egyptian warrior goddess, Bastet, which had the head of a cat. Again the Egyptian sees something to worship. With each further

Kiddush for Passover Morning

On Shabbat, begin here:

The children of Israel should keep Shabbat,
observing Shabbat throughout the generations as an eternal covenant.
It is a sign between Me and the children of Israel for all time
that the Lord made the heavens and the earth in six days,
and on the seventh day, He finished and rested.

On weekdays, begin here:

These are the set times of the Lord, holy assemblies,
which you shall proclaim at the appointed times.
And Moses told the children of Israel the appointed times of the Lord.

When Kiddush is said with a quorum of 3 or more males, 13 years or older, say the following:

Please pay attention, my masters.

Continue here:

Blessed are You, Lord, our God, King of the universe,
who creates the fruit of the vine.

קידוש ליום הפסח

On Shabbat, begin here:

וְשָׁמְרוּ בְנֵי יִשְׂרָאֵל אֶת הַשַּׁבָּת,
לַעֲשׂוֹת אֶת הַשַּׁבָּת לְדֹרֹתָם בְּרִית עוֹלָם.
בֵּינִי וּבֵין בְּנֵי יִשְׂרָאֵל אוֹת הִוא לְעֹלָם
כִּי שֵׁשֶׁת יָמִים עָשָׂה יְהֹוָה אֶת הַשָּׁמַיִם וְאֶת הָאָרֶץ,
וּבַיּוֹם הַשְּׁבִיעִי שָׁבַת וַיִּנָּפַשׁ.

On weekdays, begin here:

אֵלֶּה מוֹעֲדֵי יְהֹוָה, מִקְרָאֵי קֹדֶשׁ,
אֲשֶׁר תִּקְרְאוּ אֹתָם בְּמוֹעֲדָם.
וַיְדַבֵּר מֹשֶׁה אֶת מֹעֲדֵי יְהֹוָה אֶל בְּנֵי יִשְׂרָאֵל.

When Kiddush is said with a quorum of 3 or more males, 13 years or older, say the following:

סַבְרִי מָרָנָן.

Continue here:

בָּרוּךְ אַתָּה יְהֹוָה אֱלֹהֵינוּ מֶלֶךְ הָעוֹלָם,
בּוֹרֵא פְּרִי הַגָּפֶן.

A Prayer for Captives & Hostages

May it be Your will before You
Lord, our God, and God of our forefathers,
to strengthen, and safeguard, and protect
our brothers of the house of Israel,
the men and women held captive,
those for whom we pray.
The Holy One, blessed is He, [may He] fill them with mercy,
[may He] protect them from every trouble and distress
and from every wound and disease,
and [may He] send blessing and success in all the works of their hands,
and [may He] bring them out of darkness and obscurity,
and return them quickly to the bosom of their families,
and let us say, Amen.
Our brothers, the whole house of Israel,
those who are given over to trouble and to captivity,
[whether] they stand on the sea or on dry land,
may the Omnipresent have mercy on them,
and bring them them out of trouble to well being,
from darkness to light,
and from slavery to redemption,
now, swiftly, and at a near time,
and [let us] say, Amen.

תפילה לשבויים והחטופים

יְהִי רָצוֹן מִלְּפָנֶיךָ
יְהֹוָה אֱלֹהֵינוּ וֶאֱלֹהֵי אֲבוֹתֵינוּ,
שֶׁתְּחַזֵּק וְתִשְׁמוֹר וְתִנְצוֹר
אֶת אַחֵינוּ בֵּית יִשְׂרָאֵל,
הַשְּׁבוּיִים וְהַשְּׁבוּיוֹת,
בַּעֲבוּר שֶׁאָנוּ מִתְפַּלְּלִים בַּעֲבוּרָם.
הַקָּדוֹשׁ בָּרוּךְ הוּא יִמָּלֵא רַחֲמִים עֲלֵיהֶם,
יִשְׁמְרֵם מִכָּל צָרָה וְצוּקָה
וּמִכָּל נֶגַע וּמַחֲלָה,
וְיִשְׁלַח בְּרָכָה וְהַצְלָחָה בְּכָל מַעֲשֵׂי יְדֵיהֶם,
וְיוֹצִיאֵם מֵחֹשֶׁךְ וְצַלְמָוֶת
וִישִׁיבֵם מְהֵרָה לְחֵיק מִשְׁפְּחוֹתֵיהֶם,
וְנֹאמַר אָמֵן.
אַחֵינוּ כָּל בֵּית יִשְׂרָאֵל,
הַנְּתוּנִים בְּצָרָה וּבַשִּׁבְיָה,
הָעוֹמְדִים בֵּין בַּיָּם וּבֵין בַּיַּבָּשָׁה,
הַמָּקוֹם יְרַחֵם עֲלֵיהֶם,
וְיוֹצִיאֵם מִצָּרָה לִרְוָחָה,
וּמֵאֲפֵלָה לְאוֹרָה,
וּמִשִּׁעְבּוּד לִגְאֻלָּה,
הַשְׁתָּא בַּעֲגָלָא וּבִזְמַן קָרִיב,
וְאִמְרוּ אָמֵן.

SELECTED TRANSLITERATIONS

Ha Lakh-mah

Ha lakh-mah ahn-yah
dee ah-khah-loo ahv-hah-tah-nah beh-ahr-ah de-Meetz-rah-yeem.
Kol dikh-feen yeh-tay veh-yay-khol,
kol deetz-reekh yeh-tay veh-yeef-sakh.
Hah-shah-tah hah-khah, le-shah-nah hah-bah-ah beh-ar-ah de-Yees-rah-el.
Hah-sheh-tah ahv-day,
leh-shah-nah hah-bah-ah beh-nay kho-reen.

Continue on pages 44-45.

The Four Questions

Mah nish-tah-nah hah-lai-lah hah-zeh mee-kol hah-lay-lot?
Sheh-beh-khol hah-lay-lot ah-noo okh-leen khah-metz oo-mah-tzah,
hah-lai-la hah-zeh koo-loh mah-tzah.

Sheh-beh-khol hah-lay-lot ah-noo okh-leen sheh-ar yeh-rah-kot,
hah-lai-la hah-zeh koo-loh mah-ror.

Sheh-beh-khol hah-lay-lot ayn ah-noo maht-bee-leen ah-fee-loo peh-ahm eh-khat,
hah-lai-la hah-zeh sheh-tay peh-ah-meem.

Sheh-beh-khol hah-lay-lot ayn ah-noo ohkh-leen bayn yohsh-veen oo-vayn meh-soo-been,
hah-lai-la hah-zeh koo-lah-noo meh-soo-been.

Continue on pages 46-47.

תעתיקים נבחרים

הָא לַחְמָא עַנְיָא

הָא לַחְמָא עַנְיָא
דִּי אֲכַלוּ אַבְהָתָנָא בְּאַרְעָא דְמִצְרָיִם.
כָּל דִּכְפִין יֵיתֵי וְיֵיכֹל,
כָּל דִּצְרִיךְ יֵיתֵי וְיִפְסַח.
הָשַּׁתָּא הָכָא, לְשָׁנָה הַבָּאָה בְּאַרְעָא דְיִשְׂרָאֵל.
הָשַּׁתָּא עַבְדֵי,
לְשָׁנָה הַבָּאָה בְּנֵי חוֹרִין.

Continue on pages 44-45.

מַה נִּשְׁתַּנָּה

מַה נִּשְׁתַּנָּה הַלַּיְלָה הַזֶּה מִכָּל הַלֵּילוֹת?
שֶׁבְּכָל הַלֵּילוֹת אָנוּ אוֹכְלִין חָמֵץ וּמַצָּה,
הַלַּיְלָה הַזֶּה כֻּלּוֹ מַצָּה.

שֶׁבְּכָל הַלֵּילוֹת אָנוּ אוֹכְלִין שְׁאָר יְרָקוֹת,
הַלַּיְלָה הַזֶּה מָרוֹר.

שֶׁבְּכָל הַלֵּילוֹת אֵין אָנוּ מַטְבִּילִין אֲפִלּוּ פַּעַם אֶחָת,
הַלַּיְלָה הַזֶּה שְׁתֵּי פְעָמִים.

שֶׁבְּכָל הַלֵּילוֹת אָנוּ אוֹכְלִין בֵּין יוֹשְׁבִין וּבֵין מְסֻבִּין,
הַלַּיְלָה הַזֶּה כֻּלָּנוּ מְסֻבִּין.

Continue on pages 46-47.

Veh-hee Sheh-ahm-dah

Veh-hee sheh-ahm-dah
lah-voh-tay-noo veh-lah-noo:
Sheh-loh eh-khad beel-vahd ah-mahd ah-lay-noo leh-khah-loh-tay-noo,
eh-lah sheh-beh-khol dor vah-dor ohm-deem ah-lay-noo le-khah-loh-tay-noo,
veh-hah-Kah-dosh bah-rukh Hoo mah-tzee-lay-noo mee-yah-dahm.

Continue on pages 62-63.

The Ten Plagues

Dahm
Tzfar-dey-ah
Kee-neem
Ah-rove
Deh-veer
Sh'kheen
Bah-rahd
Ar-beh
Khoh-shekh
Mah-kaht beh-khoh-rote

Continue on pages 88-89.

Beh-tzet Yees-rah-el mee-Meetz-rah-yeem

Beh-tzet Yees-rah-el mee-Meetz-rah-yeem,
bayt Ya-ah-kov meh-ahm loh-ez,
hai-tah Yeh-hoo-dah leh-kohd-show Yees-rah-el mahm-sheh-loh-tav.
Hah-yahm rah-ah veh-yah-nos hah-yar-den yee-sove leh-ah-khor.
Heh-hah-reem rak-doo kheh-ay-leem geva-oht keev-nay tzon.

וְהִיא שֶׁעָמְדָה

וְהִיא שֶׁעָמְדָה
לַאֲבוֹתֵינוּ וְלָנוּ:
שֶׁלֹּא אֶחָד בִּלְבַד עָמַד עָלֵינוּ לְכַלּוֹתֵנוּ,
אֶלָּא שֶׁבְּכָל דּוֹר וָדוֹר עוֹמְדִים עָלֵינוּ לְכַלּוֹתֵנוּ,
וְהַקָּדוֹשׁ בָּרוּךְ הוּא מַצִּילֵנוּ מִיָּדָם.

Continue on pages 62-63.

עֶשֶׂר מַכּוֹת

דָּם
צְפַרְדֵּעַ
כִּנִּים
עָרוֹב
דֶּבֶר
שְׁחִין
בָּרָד
אַרְבֶּה
חֹשֶׁךְ
מַכַּת בְּכוֹרוֹת

Continue on pages 88-89.

בְּצֵאת יִשְׂרָאֵל מִמִּצְרָיִם

בְּצֵאת יִשְׂרָאֵל מִמִּצְרָיִם,
בֵּית יַעֲקֹב מֵעַם לֹעֵז,
הָיְתָה יְהוּדָה לְקָדְשׁוֹ יִשְׂרָאֵל מַמְשְׁלוֹתָיו.
הַיָּם רָאָה וַיָּנֹס הַיַּרְדֵּן יִסֹּב לְאָחוֹר.
הֶהָרִים רָקְדוּ כְאֵילִים גְּבָעוֹת כִּבְנֵי צֹאן.

Mah leh-khah hah-yam kee tah-noos, hah-yar-den tee-sov leh-ah-khor?
Heh-hah-reem teer-keh-doo kheh-ay-leem geh-vah-oht keev-nay tzon?
Mee-leef-nay ah-don khoo-lee ah-retz,
mee-leef-nay Eh-loh-hai Ya-ah-kov,
hah-hof-khee hah-tzoor ah-gahm mah-yeem, khah-lah-meesh le-mah-ay-no mah-yeem.

Continue on pages 106-107.

Hah-Shem Zeh-khah-rah-noo Yeh-vah-rekh

Ah-doh-nai zeh-khah-rah-noo yeh-vah-rekh.
Yeh-vah-rekh et bayt Yees-rah-el, yeh-vah-rekh et bayt Ah-hah-ron.
Yeh-vah-rekh yeh-ray Ah-doh-nai, hah-keh-tah-neem eem hah-geh-doh-leem.
Yoh-sef Ah-doh-nai ah-lei-khem, ah-lei-khem veh-al beh-nay-khem.
Beh-roo-kheem ah-tem Lah-doh-nai, oh-seh shah-mah-yeem oo-veh-ah-retz.
Hah-shah-mah-yeem shah-mah-yeem Lah-doh-nai, veh-hah-ah-retz nah-tahn leev-nay ah-dahm.
Loh hah-may-teem yeh-hah-leh-loo Yah, veh-loh kol yor-day doo-mah.
Veh-ah-nakh-noo neh-vah-rekh Yah, meh-ah-tah veh-ahd oh-lahm.
Hah-leh-loo-yah!

Continue on pages 132-133.

Mah Ah-sheev Lah-doh-nai

Mah ah-sheev lah-doh-nai kol tahg-moo-loh-hee ah-lai.
Kohs yeh-shoo-oht eh-sah oo-vah-shem Ah-doh-nai eh-krah.
Neh-dah-rai Lah-doh-nai ah-shah-lem neg-dah nah le-khol ah-moh.
Yah-kar beh-ay-nay Ah-doh-nai hah-mahv-tah lah-khah-see-dahv.
Ah-nah Ah-doh-nai kee ah-nee ahv-deh-khah, ah-nee ahv-deh-khah ben ah-mah-teh-khah.
Pee-takh-tah leh-moh-seh-rai.
Le-khah ez-bakh zeh-vakh toh-dah,

מַה לְּךָ הַיָּם כִּי תָנוּס, הַיַּרְדֵּן תִּסֹּב לְאָחוֹר?
הֶהָרִים תִּרְקְדוּ כְאֵילִים, גְּבָעוֹת כִּבְנֵי צֹאן?
מִלִּפְנֵי אָדוֹן חוּלִי אָרֶץ,
מִלִּפְנֵי אֱלוֹהַּ יַעֲקֹב,
הַהֹפְכִי הַצּוּר אֲגַם מָיִם, חַלָּמִישׁ לְמַעְיְנוֹ מָיִם.

Continue on pages 106-107.

יְהֹוָה זְכָרָנוּ יְבָרֵךְ

יְהֹוָה זְכָרָנוּ יְבָרֵךְ.
יְבָרֵךְ אֶת בֵּית יִשְׂרָאֵל, יְבָרֵךְ אֶת בֵּית אַהֲרֹן.
יְבָרֵךְ יִרְאֵי יְהֹוָה, הַקְּטַנִּים עִם הַגְּדֹלִים.
יֹסֵף יְהֹוָה עֲלֵיכֶם, עֲלֵיכֶם וְעַל בְּנֵיכֶם.
בְּרוּכִים אַתֶּם לַיהֹוָה, עֹשֵׂה שָׁמַיִם וָאָרֶץ.
הַשָּׁמַיִם שָׁמַיִם לַיהֹוָה, וְהָאָרֶץ נָתַן לִבְנֵי אָדָם.
לֹא הַמֵּתִים יְהַלְלוּ יָהּ, וְלֹא כָּל יֹרְדֵי דוּמָה.
וַאֲנַחְנוּ נְבָרֵךְ יָהּ, מֵעַתָּה וְעַד עוֹלָם.
הַלְלוּיָהּ!

Continue on pages 132-133.

מָה אָשִׁיב לַיהֹוָה

מָה אָשִׁיב לַיהֹוָה כָּל תַּגְמוּלוֹהִי עָלָי.
כּוֹס יְשׁוּעוֹת אֶשָּׂא וּבְשֵׁם יְהֹוָה אֶקְרָא.
נְדָרַי לַיהֹוָה אֲשַׁלֵּם נֶגְדָה נָּא לְכָל עַמּוֹ.
יָקָר בְּעֵינֵי יְהֹוָה הַמָּוְתָה לַחֲסִידָיו.
אָנָּה יְהֹוָה כִּי אֲנִי עַבְדֶּךָ, אֲנִי עַבְדְּךָ בֶּן אֲמָתֶךָ.
פִּתַּחְתָּ לְמוֹסֵרָי.
לְךָ אֶזְבַּח זֶבַח תּוֹדָה,

oo-veh-shem Ah-doh-nai eh-krah.
Lah-doh-nai ah-shah-lem neg-dah nah le-khol ah-moh,
beh-khatz-roht beyt Ah-doh-nai beh-toh-kheh-khee Yeh-roo-shah-lah-yeem.
Hah-leh-loo-yah!

Continue on pages 132-133.

Eh-lee Ah-tah

Eh-lee ah-tah veh-oh-deh-kah,
    Eh-lo-hai ah-roh-meh-meh-kah.
Eh-lee ah-tah veh-oh-deh-kah,
    Eh-lo-hai ah-roh-meh-meh-kah.

Hoh-doo Lah-doh-nai kee tohv,
    kee leh-oh-lahm khas-doh.
Hoh-doo Lah-doh-nai kee tohv,
    kee leh-oh-lahm khas-doh.

Continue on pages 136-137.

וּבְשֵׁם יְהֹוָה אֶקְרָא.
לַיהֹוָה אֲשַׁלֵּם נֶגְדָה נָּא לְכָל עַמּוֹ,
בְּחַצְרוֹת בֵּית יְהֹוָה בְּתוֹכֵכִי יְרוּשָׁלָיִם.
הַלְלוּיָהּ!

Continue on pages 132-133.

אֵלִי אַתָּה

אֵלִי אַתָּה וְאוֹדֶךָּ,
אֱלֹהַי אֲרוֹמְמֶךָּ.
אֵלִי אַתָּה וְאוֹדֶךָּ,
אֱלֹהַי אֲרוֹמְמֶךָּ.

הוֹדוּ לַיהֹוָה כִּי טוֹב,
כִּי לְעוֹלָם חַסְדּוֹ.
הוֹדוּ לַיהֹוָה כִּי טוֹב,
כִּי לְעוֹלָם חַסְדּוֹ.

Continue on pages 136-137.